Velma Tours

CW00550844

SLOVENIA TRAVEL GUIDE

Discover the Amazing Wonders of Ljubljana, Postojna Cave and Piran with 10 Days Perfect Itinerary for a First Timer

Table of Contents

This page was left blank intentionally

Introduction

I once set out on a trip to Slovenia that would have a lasting impact on my soul. It took place in the center of Europe, nestled between the charming Alps and the alluring Adriatic Sea. I had no idea that this tiny nation, with its stunning scenery and kind inhabitants, would provide me with an experience I would never forget.

In the charming capital city of Ljubljana, my journey began. I was in awe of the city's elegant fusion of Baroque and Art Nouveau architecture as I walked along the cobblestone streets. The Ljubljanica River, which flows gracefully through the center of the city, brought a sense of calm to the otherwise busy environment.

I was drawn to the famous Ljubljana Castle, which is perched majestically atop a hill, one sunny morning. I climbed the old stone steps of the castle, eager to explore, taking in sweeping views of the city below. My experience, however, took a surprising turn when I came across a group of locals practicing a traditional Slovenian folk dance. I soon found myself dancing alongside them and becoming fully immersed in Slovenia's rich cultural heritage after becoming mesmerized by their graceful movements and upbeat melodies.

This chance encounter gave me the motivation I needed to leave Ljubljana and discover Slovenia's other natural wonders. The untamed beauty of Triglav National Park drew me in with its clear lakes and emerald-green rivers. I set out to hike the romantic trails that wound through the park, armed only with a backpack and a spirit of adventure.

On one of these hikes, I came across Lake Bled, a stunning location that looked like it belonged in a fairy tale. The lake's emerald waters were surrounded by verdant hills, and at its center sat a small island with a charming church perched atop it. I decided to rent a traditional wooden boat called a pletna and row across the lake after becoming mesmerized by the scene.

The mellow ring of church bells and the friendly smiles of the locals welcomed me as I arrived on the island. As I ascended the 99 stone steps leading to the Assumption of

Mary Church, the island's history opened up in front of me. I found a secret world of myths and customs inside. The church's historic frescoes depicted tales of devotion and love, and the air resounded with the sound of the "wishing bell," which invited visitors to make wishes and leave heartfelt mementos behind.

I left Lake Bled behind and traveled on toward Slovenia's southwest, where the stunning coastal town of Piran awaited me. Piran exuded a timeless charm with its colorful Venetian-inspired houses and winding, narrow streets. I discovered a small café tucked away in a secret square as I wandered through its winding lanes. I went inside because of the aroma of freshly brewed coffee, and it was there that I met Ana, a local artist.

We talked for hours about creativity and the simple pleasures of life because Ana's enthusiasm for art was contagious. I was invited to her studio where she displayed her colorful works of art that were influenced by the Adriatic Sea and the coastal environment. I made a lifelong friend during our encounter in addition to learning about the beauty of art.

I considered the fortuitous events that had shaped my journey as my time in Slovenia came to an end. My visit was made extraordinary by the dance I participated in with the locals in Ljubljana, the ethereal beauty of Lake Bled, and the deep conversations I had with Ana in Piran.

Slovenia had woven itself into my being with its kindhearted people, pristine natural surroundings, and tapestry of cultural traditions. It showed me the value of welcoming chance encounters, the beauty of the present moment, and the magic that awaits those who stray from the path.

In addition to memories and a renewed sense of vigor, I said goodbye to Slovenia with the knowledge that sometimes the most extraordinary journeys are the ones we hadn't planned but were fortunate enough to take.

Welcome to Slovenia

Slovenia is a hidden gem that draws visitors with its stunning landscapes, welcoming people, and extensive cultural history. It is located in the center of Europe. This beautiful nation, frequently referred to as the "green oasis of Europe," offers a diverse tapestry of natural wonders, from snow-capped mountains and clear lakes to charming coastal towns and lush vineyards. Let's set out on a thorough journey to discover Slovenia's charm and wonders for tourists.

Our journey begins in the charming capital of Ljubljana, a bustling city that enchants tourists with its charm and magnificent architecture. You'll be welcomed by a fusion of Baroque, Art Nouveau, and Renaissance architecture as you stroll through the pedestrian-friendly streets, showcasing the city's rich history. The romantic Ljubljanica River meanders through the town, and the famed Ljubljana Castle, perched atop a hill, provides sweeping views of the area.

Triglav National Park: A Work of Nature

We come across Triglav National Park, a haven for nature lovers, as we travel northwest. This pristine wilderness is home to snow-capped mountains, lush valleys, and crystal-clear lakes. It bears the name of Mount Triglav, the highest peak in Slovenia. The majestic Lake Bohinj, encircled by the Julian Alps, invites visitors to go on hikes, go kayaking, or just relax and enjoy the peace. In the meantime, Lake Bled's emerald beauty, along with its recognizable island and medieval castle, is a picture-perfect location.

Splendors of the Coast: Piran and Portoro

As we cross over to Slovenia's Adriatic coastline, we get to the coastal town of Piran, a genuine gem. Piran exudes a Mediterranean charm that is difficult to resist with its winding, winding streets and architecture that is influenced by the Venetian style. Explore Tartini Square, the town's central square, go to St. George's Parish Church, and get lost in the labyrinthine alleys that lead to unexpected discoveries around every corner. A short distance away is

Portoro, a bustling seaside town renowned for its healing salt pans, spas, and exciting nightlife.

Into the Depths at Postojna Cave and Predjama Castle:

Going underground in Slovenia means exploring the Postojna Cave and Predjama Castle, which are both essential stops. A vast network of magnificent caverns called Postojna Cave offers a fascinating underground world adorned with stalactites and stalagmites. Take a train ride through the underground wonders with a knowledgeable guide who will reveal the secrets of this natural wonder. The fairytale-like fortress Predjama Castle, which is dramatically carved into a cliffside, is located close to the cave. Discover the castle's rooms as you gain knowledge of Erazem of Predjama's legendary exploits.

A culinary journey through the wine routes:

Slovenia is a haven for wine lovers thanks to its fertile land, which is home to some of Europe's finest vineyards. Take a trip along one of Slovenia's wine routes, like the Vipava Valley or the Jeruzalem Ormo wine region, to enjoy fine wines and the regional cuisine's culinary delights.

Experience the warm hospitality of Slovenian winemakers, who cordially invite guests to their cellars and enthusiastically share their love of winemaking.

Cultural Heritage: Traditions, Festivals, and Museums

Slovenia has a rich and varied cultural heritage, with many museums, celebrations, and customs that honor its colorful past. In Ljubljana, the Museum of Modern Art displays contemporary Slovenian art while the National Museum of Slovenia displays the nation's historical artifacts and archaeological finds. Numerous festivals that celebrate music, dance, and traditional crafts are held all year long and give visitors a full understanding of Slovenian culture.

15 Reasons to Visit Slovenian Countries

Slovenia offers a wide variety of attractions that will enthrall any traveler, from majestic Alpine peaks to charming coastal towns. In this thorough guide, we outline 15 compelling arguments for traveling to Slovenia to take in its breathtaking scenery, dynamic culture, and unforgettable experiences.

Ljubljana: A Capital of Charm and Culture: Ljubljana, Slovenia's charismatic capital, is where our journey starts. This dynamic city radiates a special fusion of old-world allure and contemporary vitality. Discover the charming Old Town, which is adorned with fine architecture, cobblestone streets, and inviting cafes. Explore the famous Ljubljana Castle, which is perched on a hilltop and provides sweeping views of the city. Visit museums, go to performances, or simply stroll along the romantic Ljubljanica River to immerse yourself in the city's cultural delights.

A Fairytale Destination: Lake Bled

A scene from a fairytale comes to life at Lake Bled with its emerald-green waters, a small island topped by a church, and a medieval castle perched on a cliff. Travel to the island on a traditional wooden pletna boat, visit the Assumption of Mary Church and ring the "wishing bell" to invoke luck. From Bled Castle, take in the expansive views while indulging in the world-famous Bled cream cake—a delectable treat not to be missed.

Triglav National Park: A Playground in Nature

Triglav National Park is a paradise just waiting to be discovered by nature lovers. This stunning wilderness is home to the Julian Alps and Mount Triglav, the highest peak in Slovenia. Wander through picturesque valleys, come across cascading waterfalls, and take in the beauty of lakes with pristine water like Lake Bohinj and Lake Jasna. Invigorating outdoor pursuits like mountaineering, paragliding, and whitewater rafting are also possible in the park.

The Adriatic coast of Slovenia is lined with charming towns, but Piran stands out as a true coastal gem. Visitors are enthralled by this charming medieval town's winding streets, pastel-colored homes, and breathtaking coastal views. Discover Tartini Square, go to St. George's Parish Church and eat fresh seafood at neighborhood eateries. Visit the historical city walls for panoramic views or unwind on one of the many stunning beaches that line the coastline.

Postojna Cave: A Subterranean World

Explore Postojna Cave, one of the most alluring underground wonders in existence. Take a train ride through this vast network of caves and take in the fascinating stalactite, stalagmite, and other limestone formations. Investigate the 13th-century Predjama Castle, which is a fortress built into a cave mouth and is close to the cave. Learn about the stories of nobles and knights that surround this fascinating castle.

The Lipizzaner horses are raised at the Lipica Stud Farm.

Visit the Lipica Stud Farm, the birthplace of the renowned Lipizzaner horses, to learn more about Slovenia's equestrian history. Watch these elegant white horses perform with grace at the Lipica Classical Riding School. Experience the tranquil beauty of the surrounding countryside while learning about the history of the breed on a guided tour.

Adventure in pristine beauty: The Soa Valley is a haven for outdoor enthusiasts thanks to its emerald-green Soa River. Experience exhilarating sports in the clear waters, such as whitewater rafting, kayaking, canyoning, and fly fishing. Hike through the picturesque valley, which is bordered by the Julian Alps, to find secret waterfalls and quaint alpine hamlets.

Ptuj: A Trip Through Time:

One of Slovenia's oldest towns, Ptuj is known for its extensive history and well-preserved medieval architecture, allowing visitors to travel back in time. Explore the massive Ptuj Castle, go to the Ptuj Ormo Regional Museum, and stroll through the Old Town's winding streets while taking in the quaint ambiance. Be sure to attend the Ptuj Carnival, one of Europe's oldest continuously held carnivals, which lines the streets with vibrant parades and joyful revelry.

Slovenia's wine capital is Maribor.

Indulge your senses in Maribor, the picturesque wine-growing region's capital and Slovenia's capital of wine. Visit the Old Vine House, which is home to the oldest grapevine in the world, and learn about the burgeoning wine industry through tours and tastings of vineyards. A thriving cultural scene is also present in the city, which includes theaters, art galleries, and the Maribor Symphony Orchestra.

Alpine Majesty: Julian Alps:

The Julian Alps provide a wide range of options for those looking for Alpine adventures. Hike the trails that take you to breathtaking views, such as the breathtaking Seven Triglav Lakes Valley. The area becomes a winter wonderland in the winter, drawing skiers and snowboarders to well-known resorts like Kranjska Gora and Vogel.

Discover the historical significance of the Soa Valley town of Kobarid, which was a key player in World War I, in Kobarid: A Historical Hub. Investigate the Kobarid Museum, which is devoted to the Soa Front, to learn more about the challenges that soldiers faced. Visit the close-by, magnificent Kozjak Waterfall, a hidden gem amidst lush vegetation.

Kocjan Caves: A Underground Wonder

Explore the ethereal Kocjan Caves, a UNESCO World Heritage site that is home to one of the world's largest underground canyons. Cross suspended bridges to see the raging Reka River carving through the underground spaces. This cave system is a must-visit for nature lovers due to its distinctive geology and captivating formations.

Velika Planina: Alpine Serenity: Velika Planina is a mountain plateau in the Kamnik-Savinja Alps. It is the perfect place to get away from the hustle and bustle of the big city. This idyllic alpine pasture, which is reachable by cable car or hiking trails, offers peace, beautiful hikes, and a look into the traditional herder's way of life. Admire the charming herdsmen's cottages and indulge in the hearty regional fare.

A Nature Lover's Paradise: Vintgar Gorge

Visit Vintgar Gorge, a breathtaking natural wonder close to Lake Bled, to witness the unbridled power of nature. Travel through confined spaces and beneath majestic waterfalls while strolling along wooden walkways suspended above the raging Radovna River. You will be in awe of the gorge's vivid green colors and its surreal atmosphere.

Slovenian Food: A Delight for the Tastebuds

Slovenian food offers a delightful fusion of flavors and reflects the nation's varied cultural influences. Try traditional foods like ganci (buckwheat spoonbread), potica (rolled pastry with a variety of fillings), and truklji. Try some Slovenian wines, including some of the regional selections like Refosco and Teran. Don't pass up the chance to sample delicious honey made in the centuries-old beekeeping tradition.

This page was left blank intentionally

7 interesting Facts About Slovenia

I will delve into seven fascinating facts about Slovenia in this comprehensive guide, revealing its rich history, natural wonders, cultural heritage, and more. Let's set out on a quest for knowledge and discover this gem's charms.

1. **A Land of Breathtaking Beau**ty: Slovenia is known as the "green oasis of Europe" for its astounding variety of natural landscapes. Even though it is small, the nation is home to a variety of treasures, such as the Julian Alps, Triglav National Park, charming lakes like Bled and Bohinj, and the picturesque Soa Valley. Slovenia's natural beauty is a haven for outdoor enthusiasts and nature lovers alike, with everything from snow-capped mountains to rolling hills, dense forests to clear rivers.

2. Ljubljana, the capital of Slovenia, was named the prestigious 2016 recipient of the title of Europe's Green Capital. The city's dedication to sustainable practices,

environmental protection, and quality of life is demonstrated by this award. Ljubljana is distinguished by its wide sidewalks, an abundance of greenery, and an extensive public transportation system. The city's eco-friendly policies, waste management systems, cycling infrastructure, and other sustainable initiatives have won praise from around the world and added to the city's lively and livable atmosphere.

3. **A Bridge of Architectural Styles**: Slovenia's rich history and numerous cultural influences are reflected in the country's architectural landscape. You can find a harmonious blending of architectural styles all over the country, from Baroque churches to Art Nouveau structures, as well as medieval castles and Roman ruins. The Triple Bridge, Preseren Square, and Ljubljana Castle are examples of the city's outstanding architecture from various eras. Additionally, Maribor has lovely examples of Renaissance and Art Nouveau architecture, and the coastal town of Piran boasts well-preserved Venetian Gothic architecture. Discovering Slovenia's architectural treasures is like traveling through time and discovering history's many facets.

4. The world's oldest grapevine, also known as "Stara trta" or the Old Vine, is proudly grown in Slovenia. This venerable vine, which can be found in Maribor, has endured wars, phylloxera, and shifting topography for more than 400 years. The Old Vine House, a museum and a symbol of the area's long history of winemaking, is located next to the vine. Visitors can discover the origins of winemaking, sample regional wines, and take part in cultural activities centered on this enduring representation of viticulture.

5. **A Peaceful Nation**: Slovenia is one of the few nations in the world without an army, which gives it a special place in the world. Slovenia adopted a diplomatic and cooperative stance in its international relations after gaining independence from Yugoslavia in 1991. Slovenia's proactive participation in international organizations, such as the United Nations and the European Union, is a testament to its dedication to peace. The absence of armed conflicts enables the nation to allocate resources to other industries like sustainable development, education, and culture.

6. The renowned Lipizzaner horses were first bred at Slovenia's Lipica Stud Farm, making them one of the continent's oldest horse breeds. The stud farm, which was established in 1580, has preserved the illustrious pedigree of these graceful white horses. At the Lipica Classical Riding School, visitors can see demonstrations of classical dressage and tour the farm's expansive grounds, which are home to over 300 Lipizzaner horses. The Lipizzaner breed has a significant cultural and historical significance and is closely linked to Slovenia's and its neighboring nations' equestrian traditions.

7. **A Linguistic Bridge**: Slovenian, the nation's official tongue, is a distinctive and fascinating linguistic link. It is a member of the South Slavic family of languages, which also includes Bosnian, Croatian, and Serbian. Slovenian is the only Slavic language to use a dual grammatical number in addition to the singular and plural, despite having a small population. The melodic tones of Slovenian are spoken in a variety of dialects,

reflecting the country's regional diversity. This linguistic oddity adds to Slovenia's allure.

The Best Way to Move Around in Slovenia

Each mode of transportation has advantages and disadvantages, from quick public transportation to the freedom of renting a car. In this chapter, I will examine the best ways to get around Slovenia, taking into account aspects like cost, convenience, impact on the environment, and overall experience. Let's explore the options in more detail so you can choose wisely for your Slovenian adventure.

Trains and Buses as Public Transportation

Slovenia has a well-developed public transportation system, making trains and buses a practical and environmentally friendly means of travel. Pros and cons are listed below:

Pros:

- Trains and buses connect Slovenia's major cities, towns, and tourist destinations, providing convenient access to both well-known and off-the-beaten-path locations.

- **Cost-Effective**: For solo travelers or small groups, public transportation is frequently less expensive than car rentals.

- **Reliability**: Slovenian trains and buses are renowned for their punctuality and dependability, which guarantees that you arrive at your destination on time.

- **Train routes,** like the Bohinj Railway, offer picturesque views of Slovenia's breathtaking landscapes, making for an interesting and enjoyable travel experience.

Cons:

- **Limited Flexibility**: Public transportation operates on predetermined schedules that might not always coincide with your preferred route. Your exploration may be constrained by this restriction, which calls for careful planning.

- Reaching remote or rural areas may require additional transfers or have fewer service options, despite the public transportation system's extensive network.

- Popular tourist destinations may become congested during peak travel times, which limits the number of seats available on trains and buses.

- **Pricing:** Train and bus tickets in Slovenia are typically reasonably priced. Express trains and regional buses, for example, have different prices depending on the route taken and the type of service provided. A one-way train ticket from Ljubljana to Bled typically costs between €6 and €10, whereas a bus ticket for the same route costs between €5 and €8. Children, seniors, and students can frequently get discounts.

Renting a Car:

Traveling independently and at your own pace is made possible in Slovenia by renting a car. Pros and cons are listed below:

Pros:

- **Flexibility**: Having a car gives you the freedom to plan your route, travel to distant locations, and find undiscovered attractions. Spend as much time as you'd like in each location and tailor your journey to your preferences.
- **Convenience**: Renting a car allows you to travel door-to-door without having to carry your luggage on public transportation or adhere to set schedules.
- **Rural Accessibility**: Renting a car makes it simpler to reach outlying areas and natural attractions if you intend to explore Slovenia's countryside.

Cons:

- **Cost:** Considering rental fees, fuel costs, tolls, and parking costs, using a rental car in Slovenia can be more expensive than using the public transportation system.
- **Parking difficulties**: Finding parking spaces in well-known tourist destinations like Ljubljana or Bled can be difficult and may entail paying for parking or having a limited supply during high season.
- **Impact on the Environment**: Increasing carbon emissions from personal auto travel raise

environmental concerns. Your ecological footprint can be reduced by choosing sustainable alternatives like public transportation or car-sharing services.

- **Price**: The cost of renting a car in Slovenia varies depending on the rental agency, the length of the rental, and the type of vehicle. A day's worth of renting a small economy car typically costs between €30 and €50. Your budget should account for extra expenses like insurance, fuel, tolls, and parking fees.

Cycling:

Slovenia is a great country to tour on two wheels because of its beautiful landscapes and well-maintained cycling routes. Pros and cons are listed below:

Pros:

- Cycling is both physically active and environmentally friendly, allowing you to take in Slovenia's natural beauty while lowering your carbon footprint.

- Slovenia has many scenic cycling routes, including the well-known Parenzana Trail, which passes through quaint towns and lovely countryside.
- **Freedom and Flexibility**: Cycling allows you the freedom to travel at your own pace, stop for pictures, and veer off the beaten path.

Cons:

- Cycling calls for a certain level of physical fitness and stamina, particularly when negotiating hilly or mountainous terrain.
- **Limited Range**: Cycling may place restrictions on your range and ability to travel to far-off locations within Slovenia, depending on your level of fitness and the length of your trip.
- **Weather consideration**s: During colder or rainier seasons, the weather can affect whether cycling is feasible and enjoyable.
- **Price**: Renting a bicycle in Slovenia is a popular choice if you don't have your own. Prices change based on the length of the rental and the type of bike. Standard bicycles typically cost between €10

and €20 per day to rent, whereas electric bicycles can run between €20 and €40 per day.

30 Top Dos and Don'ts in Slovenia

You can ensure that your time in Slovenia is respectful and rewarding by adhering to these 30 major dos and don'ts. Accept the traditions of the area, interact with nature, and become fully immersed in the rich cultural heritage. 30 things you should know before visiting Slovenia are listed below:

Dos:

- Embrace Greetings and Politeness: Do extend a handshake and make eye contact when you greet people.
- Use "Dober dan" (Good day) as your default salutation.
- When addressing people, use respectful pronouns like "gospod" (sir) and "gospa" (madam).

- Respect cultural customs by taking off your shoes before entering a home.
- When visiting churches or monasteries, show respect by dressing modestly.
- Discover Slovenia's Culinary Delights: Try some traditional foods like "potica" (rolled pastry), "kranjska klobasa" (Carniolan sausage), and "truklji" (rolled dumplings) as well as other delectable fares.
- Discover the rich wine culture by tasting regional wines like Teran and Refosco.
- Consider the Environment: When hiking or exploring Slovenia's pristine landscapes, respect nature and leave no trace.
- Respect protected areas and stick to designated trails.
- Participate in sustainable tourism by buying genuine Slovenian goods and crafts to support regional producers, artisans, and farmers.
- Select environmentally friendly modes of transportation, and be aware of your energy usage.
- Learn a few basic Slovene words and phrases to communicate with locals and to express gratitude,

such as "Hvala" (thank you), "Prosim" (please), and "Oprostite" (excuse me).

- Visit Ljubljana Castle for sweeping views of the city as you explore this charming capital of Slovenia.
- Take a stroll along the lovely Ljubljanica River and pedal your way through the bustling city center.
- Visit Lake Bled and Lake Bohinj to marvel at these two breathtaking natural wonders.
- Go to Bled Island by boat and ring the lucky bell there.
- Explore Postojna Cave and Predjama Castle: Postojna Cave is a magical underground world with fascinating formations.
- Visit Predjama Castle, a stunning fortress carved out of a cliff.
- Do embrace the beauty of the Julian Alps by going on a hike, a bike ride, or a ski trip in Triglav National Park.
- Views from Slovenia's highest peak, Mount Triglav, are breathtaking.
- Enjoy the Adriatic Coast's Beauty: Unwind in the quaint coastal towns of Piran and Portoro.

- Savor delicious fresh seafood dishes while taking in the sun, sand, and sea.
- Explore Ptuj, the oldest town in Slovenia, which is renowned for its illustrious past and lively festivals.
- To experience the regional wine culture, go to Ptuj Castle and the Ptuj Wine Cellar.
- Experience the Thermal Spas: Take advantage of Slovenia's rich tradition of thermal spas by relaxing in the therapeutic waters of Terme ate, Terme Olimia, or Rogaka Slatina.
- Give yourself the gift of revitalizing spa services and wellness activities.
- Enjoy Outdoor Activities: Take advantage of Slovenia's varied landscapes by participating in outdoor activities like rafting, kayaking, canyoning, or paragliding.
- Participate in Festivals and Traditions: Get involved in Slovenia's cultural events, such as the Kurentovanje Carnival in Ptuj or the annual "koline" (pig slaughter) celebrations.

Don'ts:

- Don't Forget to Validate Your Tickets: To avoid penalties, remember to validate your bus or train tickets as soon as you board.
- Utilize the ticket checkers found in the vehicles or at the stations.
- Don't Rush Through Ljubljana's City Center: Take your time when you are in Ljubljana. Explore its quaint streets, lively markets, and secret nooks at your own pace.
- Don't Expect Rush Service: Don't anticipate hurried service in cafes or restaurants. Enjoy your leisurely meal because Slovenian culture values a laid-back attitude.
- Avoid Being Excessively Loud or Disruptive: Slovenians value peace, so refrain from being excessively loud or disruptive in public areas.
- Don't Forget Cash for Rural Areas: In rural or small-town settings, don't rely solely on card payments. Keep some cash on hand because some businesses might only take cash.
- Leave No Trace: Do not litter or abandon any trash. Respect the environment and properly dispose of waste.

- Don't Underestimate Mountain Safety: Be aware of the difficulties presented by the mountains. Be prepared, observe safety precautions, and check the weather before hiking or climbing.

- Respect Sacred Sites: It is disrespectful to take pictures or make loud noises inside religious buildings.

- Don't Make Disrespectful Remarks About National Symbols: Avoid making disparaging remarks or jokes about national emblems like the Slovenian flag or coat of arms.

- Limit Your Exploration to Less Popular Areas: For a more genuine experience, broaden your horizons and explore lesser-known regions, towns, and villages in addition to popular tourist destinations.

- Avoid touching or disturbing wildlife, especially in areas that are protected. Respect the wildlife's natural habitat and keep your distance when watching them.

- Don't Overtip: You shouldn't feel compelled to give excessive tips. While leaving a tip is always appreciated, 10% is usually enough in restaurants.

- Avoid Wearing Revealing Clothing in Churches: Avoid wearing revealing clothing while touring monasteries or churches. Respect religious customs by dressing modestly.

- Avoid assuming Slovenes Do not assume that Slovenians are Russian-speaking. Although some people may speak English or German, Slovenian is the official language, so it's polite to learn a few fundamental Slovenian phrases.

Do I Need a Visa to Visit Slovenia?

To ensure a simple and hassle-free trip, it is essential to comprehend the visa requirements if you are planning a trip to this beautiful country. In this chapter, I will cover Slovenia's visa requirements, including exceptions, types of visas, application procedures, and significant factors. To answer the question **"Do I need a visa to visit Slovenia?"** let's get into the specifics.

Short-term Visitor Visa Exemptions:

Slovenia adheres to the visa rules established by the Schengen Agreement as a member of the Schengen Area. These rules exempt citizens of particular nations from the need for a visa for brief visits (up to 90 days within 180 days). Visas are typically not required for the following groups to visit Slovenia:

Citizens of member nations of the European Union (EU) and the European Free Trade Association (EFTA), such as those in Germany, France, Italy, the United Kingdom,

Switzerland, and Norway, are eligible to enter Slovenia with a valid national ID card or passport.

Countries that have ratified the Schengen Agreement include the United States, Canada, Australia, New Zealand, Japan, South Korea, and many others. Citizens of these nations are eligible to travel to Slovenia without a visa for up to 90 days within a 180-day window.

Before traveling, it is crucial to confirm the most recent information and the status of your particular country's visa exemption as rules can change. Current information can be obtained from the Slovenian Ministry of Foreign Affairs or the Slovenian Embassy or Consulate in your country.

If you are a national of a nation that isn't exempt from the need for a visa or if you intend to stay in Slovenia for more than 90 days, you'll need to apply for a Schengen visa. With a Schengen visa, you can freely move around Slovenia and the other 25 European nations that make up the Schengen Area.

Schengen Visa Types:

There are various Schengen visas available depending on why you're traveling, including:

a. Visa for tourism (Type C Schengen Visa):

- You will require a tourist visa if you are traveling to Slovenia for leisure, sightseeing, or seeing friends and family.
- This visa has a maximum 90-day validity window within a 180-day window.

b. A business visa (Type C Schengen Visa):

- You will need a business visa if you are going to Slovenia to conduct business, attend conferences, or engage in professional activities.
- The business visa allows a stay of up to 90 days during 180 days, much like the tourist visa.

c. The national visa (D visa)

- A national visa (D visa) is required if you intend to stay in Slovenia for some time longer than 90 days or if you have specific objectives like employment, study, or family reunion.
- Subject to the particular conditions and requirements of your stay, the national visa enables you to stay in Slovenia for an extended period.

Obtaining a Schengen visa

To obtain a Schengen visa to travel to Slovenia, take the following general actions:

a. **Determine the appropriate visa type** (tourist, business, or national visa) based on the reason for and length of your visit.

b. **Fill out the application:** You can get the Schengen visa application form from the Slovenian Embassy or Consulate or online from their official site. Accurately complete the form and include all necessary details.

c. **Compile the required paperwork**: Prepare the necessary supporting documentation, which may include a current passport, two passport-sized photos, a travel itinerary, travel insurance, proof of lodging, proof of financial ability, and any other paperwork unique to your visa type (such as an invitation letter for a business visa).

d. **Make an appointment**: To make an appointment to submit your visa application, get in touch with the Slovenian Embassy/Consulate or the visa application center in your nation.

e. **Submit your application**: Show up for the appointment and present the required paperwork, including your visa application. Pay the appropriate visa fee, which varies based on your nationality and the type of visa you have.

f. **Show up for the interview**: In some circumstances, a visa applicant may be required to attend an interview. Be prepared to respond to inquiries about the reason for your visit, your financial situation, and your travel schedule.

g. **Follow the application's progress**: Following submission, you can monitor the application's status using the designated tracking system offered by the Slovenian Embassy/Consulate or the visa application center.

h. **Pick up your visa**: After your visa application has been approved, go to the Slovenian Embassy or Consulate or the designated visa application center to pick up your visa.

Important Points:

a. **Apply early:** Because visa processing times can vary, it is advised to apply for your Schengen visa well in advance of the dates you intend to travel. It is advised to submit your application at least 2-3 months before your planned departure.

b. Travel insurance: Make sure you have travel insurance that satisfies the requirements for Schengen visas, including the minimum amount of coverage for medical emergencies and repatriation.

c. **Financial means proof**: Be ready to demonstrate that you have the resources necessary to support yourself while visiting Slovenia. Depending on your circumstances, this might include bank statements, income certificates, or sponsorship letters.

d. **Medical exams**: A medical exam or particular vaccinations may be necessary, depending on your country of residence and the length of your stay. Consult the Slovenian Embassy or Consulate or a visa application center for the requirements.

e. **Multiple-entry visa**: If you intend to travel to other Schengen nations, think about requesting a visa that permits multiple entries and exits from the Schengen Area.

This page was left blank intentionally

Visa Entry Requirement for Slovenia

Slovenia draws tourists from all over the world with its beautiful landscapes, extensive cultural history, and friendly people. Understanding the visa entry requirements is crucial if you're planning a trip to this beautiful country to guarantee a hassle-free trip. In this chapter, I will cover Slovenia's visa entry requirements, including visa-exempt nations, visa categories, application procedures, and significant factors. Let's get into the specifics so you have a clear understanding of Slovenia's visa entry requirements.

Countries exempt from visa requirements: Slovenia abides by the visa rules established by the Schengen Agreement as a member of the Schengen Area. These rules exempt citizens of specific nations from the need for a visa for brief visits (up to 90 days within 180 days) into Slovenia. Visas are typically not required for the following groups to visit Slovenia:

a. Citizens of the European Union (EU) and the European Free Trade Association (EFTA)

- With a valid national ID card or passport, citizens of EU member states—including those from Germany, France, Italy, Spain, and other nations—can enter Slovenia.
- Slovenia can also be entered with a valid national ID card or passport from an EFTA member state, such as Switzerland, Norway, Iceland, or Liechtenstein.

b. States that have ratified the Schengen Agreement:

- Non-EU/EFTA nationals who have signed the Schengen Agreement are eligible for visa-free entry into Slovenia for up to 90 days within 180 days. The United States, Canada, Australia, New Zealand, Japan, South Korea, and many more are a few of these nations.
- While citizens of these nations are not required to have a visa to enter Slovenia, they must still have a valid travel document (passport or ID card) that is

valid for at least three months after the date of their intended departure from Slovenia.

- Regulations regarding visa exemption are subject to change, so it is advisable to confirm the most recent details before departing. Current information on visa exemptions can be obtained from the Slovenian Ministry of Foreign Affairs or the Slovenian Embassy or Consulate in your home country.
- If you are a national of a nation that isn't exempt from the need for a visa or if you intend to stay in Slovenia for more than 90 days, you'll need to apply for a Schengen visa. With a Schengen visa, you can freely move around Slovenia and the other 25 European nations that make up the Schengen Area.

Schengen Visa Types:

Various Schengen visas are available, depending on the reason for and length of your visit:

a. Unified Schengen Visa (USV), also known as a "C" visa:

- This visa is appropriate for quick trips for leisure, business, or to see friends and family.
- The USV permits a stay of up to 90 days during 180 days.

b. National Visa (NV), also known as a "D" visa

- A national visa is required if you intend to stay in Slovenia for some time longer than 90 days or if you have specific objectives such as employment, study, or family reunion.
- The NV is typically issued for a longer period and calls for additional paperwork that is particular to your reason for staying.

Obtaining a Schengen visa

To obtain a Schengen visa to enter Slovenia, take the following general actions:

a. Determine the type of visa:

- Choose between a national visa or a uniform Schengen visa depending on the reason for and length of your visit.
- Depending on the number of times you intend to travel within the Schengen Area, decide whether you require a single-entry or multiple-entry visa.

b. Compile the necessary paperwork:

- Obtain a Schengen visa application form by visiting the Slovenian Embassy or Consulate's website. Fill out the form completely and with the necessary details.
- Prepare the necessary supporting documentation, which may include a current passport, two passport-sized photos taken within the last year, a travel itinerary, evidence of lodging, travel insurance,

proof of financial ability, and any other paperwork unique to your visa type (such as an invitation letter for a business visa or an acceptance letter for a study visa).

- Make sure that each document complies with the requirements for validity, size, and format.

c. Make a reservation:

- To make an appointment for submitting your visa application, get in touch with the Slovenian Embassy/Consulate or the designated visa application center in your nation.
- Some nations might ask you to make an online appointment with a visa application center.

d. Pay a visit to the appointment and submit your application:

- Attend the appointment at the Slovenian Embassy or Consulate or the designated center for visa applications.
- Send in your completed visa application form and the required paperwork.

- Pay the appropriate visa fee, which varies based on your nationality and the type of visa you have. The payment receipt should be kept for future use.

e. **Gathering biometric information:**

- In some circumstances, gathering biometric information (fingerprints and a photo) is necessary as part of the visa application procedure. The information is typically gathered at the Slovenian Embassy or Consulate or the visa application center. Follow up on the application:
- After submitting your application, you can keep track of its status using the special tracking system offered by the Slovenian Embassy or Consulate or the visa application center.
- This enables you to stay up to date on the status of your application and, if necessary, any additional requirements.

g. **Enter a job interview:**

- A visa application interview might be necessary in some circumstances. The consular representative can now evaluate the reason for your visit and compile any additional information.

- Be ready to respond to inquiries about your intended destination, accommodations, finances, and travel schedule.

h. **Visa approval and payment:**

- You will be informed by the Slovenian Embassy/Consulate or the visa application center once a decision has been made regarding your visa application.
- Pick up your visa from the designated location if it has been approved. If your visa application is rejected, you will be given a written justification for the decision.

Important Points to Keep in Mind

a. **Apply ahead of time:**

- Given that the processing time for visas can vary, it is advised to apply for your Schengen visa well in advance of the dates you intend to travel.

It is advised to submit your application at least two to three months before your planned departure.

b. Full-coverage travel insurance

- You must have travel insurance that satisfies the prerequisites for a Schengen visa, with a minimum level of protection of 30,000 euros for unexpected medical expenses, hospitalization, and return home.
- Make sure that the duration of your stay in the Schengen Area is covered by your insurance policy.

c. Evidence of financial resources

- Be prepared to show evidence that you have the money to cover your stay in Slovenia. Depending on your circumstances, this might include bank statements, income certificates, or sponsorship letters.

d. Passport's remaining validity:

- At least three months must pass after your intended departure date from Slovenia for your passport to remain valid.
- The passport must also have two blank pages for visa stamps and be from within the last ten years of issue.

e. **Consular authority:**

- At the Slovenian Embassy or Consulate in the nation where you are legally residing, apply for a Schengen visa. If Slovenia is not represented in your nation, you might need to apply at the embassy or consulate of the closest Schengen nation that has a representation agreement with Slovenia.

f. **History of prior Schengen visas:**

- Make sure you have complied with all visa requirements, including timely departure from the Schengen Area, if you have previously held a Schengen visa. A visa overstay may hurt a future visa application.

g. **Additional conditions**

- Additional requirements might be necessary for you if you're traveling with minors, engaging in a particular activity, or going for medical treatment. For comprehensive information, speak with the Slovenian Embassy/Consulate or the visa application center.

List of Countries That Are Visa Exempt in Slovenia

You can find a complete list of nations that don't need a visa to visit Slovenia in this chapter. This information will help you determine whether you need to apply for a visa or if you can travel to Slovenia without one, regardless of whether you are a citizen of an EU member state, an EFTA country, or a non-EU/EFTA country.

Visa-free nations:

Slovenia abides by the visa policies established by the Schengen Agreement as a member of the Schengen Area. Slovenia is one of the countries that can travel without a visa thanks to the Schengen Agreement. Visas are typically not needed for the following traveler categories to visit Slovenia for brief stays (up to 90 days in 180 days):

a. Citizens of the European Union (EU) and the European Free Trade Association (EFTA)

All EU members are eligible to visit Slovenia without a visa if they have a valid national ID card or passport.

b. **EFTA Members**: Holders of a valid national ID card or passport from an EFTA Member State (Switzerland, Norway, Iceland, and Liechtenstein) may enter Slovenia without a visa.

Non-EU/EFTA nations with agreements granting visa exemptions:

a. **Albanian** nationals are not required to have a visa to enter Slovenia for up to 90 days during 180 days.

b. Andorra: Within 180 days, Andorran nationals are permitted 90 days of visa-free travel to Slovenia.

c. **Antigua and Barbuda**: Within a 180-day window, citizens of Antigua and Barbuda are eligible for a 90-day visa-free stay in Slovenia.

d. **Argentine nationals** are exempt from the visa requirement for up to 90 days within 180 days in Slovenia.

e. **Australia**: Australian nationals can travel to Slovenia without a visa for up to 90 days within a 180-day window.

f. **Bahamas**: Within a 180-day window, Bahamas nationals are permitted a 90-day visa-free stay in Slovenia.

g. **Barbados:** Within a 180-day window, Barbadian nationals are permitted up to 90 days of visa-free travel to Slovenia.

h. **Bosnia and Herzegovina:** Within 180 days, Bosnia and Herzegovina nationals are permitted entry into Slovenia without a visa for up to 90 days.

I. **Brazil:** Brazilian nationals are eligible for a 180-day visa-free stay in Slovenia for up to 90 days.

J. **Brunei:** Within a 180-day window, Bruneian nationals are permitted up to 90 days of visa-free travel to Slovenia.

k. **Canada**: Canadian nationals can travel to Slovenia without a visa for up to 90 days within a 180-day window.

l. **Chileans** do not need a visa to enter Slovenia for up to 90 days during 180 days.

m. **Colombia:** Within a 180-day window, Colombian nationals are permitted up to 90 days of visa-free travel to Slovenia.

n. **Costa Rica**: Costa Rican nationals do not need a visa to enter Slovenia for up to 90 days during 180 days.

o. **Dominica:** Within a 180-day window, Dominican nationals are permitted a 90-day visa-free stay in Slovenia.

p. **El Salvador**: Within a 180-day window, El Salvadorean nationals are permitted up to 90 days of visa-free travel to Slovenia.

q. Grenada: Within 180 days, citizens of Grenada are permitted entry to Slovenia without a visa for up to 90 days.

r. Guatemalan nationals can travel to Slovenia for up to 90 days within a 180-day window without a visa.

s. Holy See (Vatican City State) nationals are exempt from Slovenian visa requirements for up to 90 days for 180 days.

t. **Hondurans** can travel to Slovenia without a visa for up to 90 days during 180 days.

u. **Hong Kong** (Special Administrative Region of China) residents are exempt from visa requirements to enter Slovenia for up to 90 days within a 180-day window.

v. **Israel v. Slovenia**: Within a 180-day window, Israeli nationals are permitted up to 90 days of visa-free travel to Slovenia.

Japan citizens do not need a visa to enter Slovenia for up to 90 days during 180 days.

x. **Kosovo**: Citizens of Kosovo are not required to obtain a visa to enter Slovenia for up to 90 days within a 180-day window.

y. **Macao** (Special Administrative Region of China): Citizens of Macao are exempt from the visa requirement for up to 90 days during 180 days of travel to Slovenia.

z. **Macedonia** (North Macedonia): Within a 180-day window, Macedonians can travel to Slovenia without a visa for up to 90 days.

Malaysian nationals are exempt from the visa requirement for up to 90 days within 180 days in Slovenia.

bb. **Mauritius:** Within a 180-day window, Mauritius nationals are permitted up to 90 days of visa-free travel to Slovenia.

cc. **Mexico**: Mexican nationals can travel to Slovenia without a visa for up to 90 days within a 180-day window.

dd. **Moldovan** nationals can travel to Slovenia for up to 90 days within a 180-day window without a visa.

ee. **Monaco** residents don't need a visa to visit Slovenia for up to 90 days during 180 days.

ff. **Montenegro**: Within a 180-day window, Montenegrin nationals are permitted entry to Slovenia for up to 90 days without a visa.

gg. **New Zealand**: Within 180 days, New Zealanders are permitted a 90-day visa-free stay in Slovenia.

hh. **Nicaraguan** nationals are not required to have a visa to enter Slovenia for up to 90 days during 180 days.

ii. Visa-free travel is permitted for up to 90 days within 180 days for citizens of Palau.

jj. **Panama**: Panamanian nationals can travel to Slovenia for up to 90 days within a 180-day window without a visa.

kk. **Paraguay**: Within a 180-day window, Paraguayan nationals are permitted up to 90 days of visa-free travel to Slovenia.

ll. **Peru:** People from Peru do not need a visa to enter Slovenia for up to 90 days during 180 days.

mm. **Saint Kitts and Nevis**: Within 180 days, visitors from Saint Kitts and Nevis are permitted a 90-day visa-free stay in Slovenia.

nn. **Saint Lucia**: Saint Lucian nationals do not need a visa to visit Slovenia for up to 90 days during 180 days.

oo. **Saint Vincent and the Grenadine**s: Saint Vincent and the Grenadines nationals do not require a visa to enter Slovenia for up to 90 days during 180 days.

pp. **Samoan** nationals can travel to Slovenia for up to 90 days within 180 days without a visa.

qq. **San Marino:** San Marino nationals are permitted up to 90 days of visa-free entry into Slovenia within 180 days.

rr. **Serbian** nationals are not required to have a visa to enter Slovenia for up to 90 days during 180 days.

ss. **Seychelles**: Within a 180-day window, Seychelles nationals are permitted 90-day visa-free stays in Slovenia.

tt. **Singapore**: Within 180 days, Singaporeans are permitted up to 90 days of visa-free travel to Slovenia.

uu. **South Korea**: South Korean nationals do not need a visa to enter Slovenia for up to 90 days during 180 days.

vv. Taiwan: Within a 180-day window, citizens of Taiwan may travel to Slovenia for up to 90 days without a visa.

ww. Timor-Leste nationals do not need a visa to visit Slovenia for up to 90 days during 180 days.

xx. **Tonga**: Tonga nationals can travel to Slovenia without a visa for up to 90 days within a 180-day window.

yy. **Trinidad and Tobago**: Within 180 days, citizens of Trinidad and Tobago are permitted a 90-day visa-free stay in Slovenia.

zz. **Ukraine**: Within a 180-day window, Ukrainian nationals are permitted up to 90 days of visa-free travel to Slovenia.

aaa. **United Arab Emirates:** UAE nationals do not need a visa to enter Slovenia for up to 90 days during 180 days.

bbb. **United States of America**: American nationals are permitted a 90-day visa-free stay in Slovenia within 180 days.

ccc. **Uruguay**: Within 180 days, Uruguayan nationals are permitted up to 90 days of visa-free travel to Slovenia.

ddd. **Vanuatu**: Within 180 days, citizens of Vanuatu may enter Slovenia without a visa for up to 90 days.

eee. **Venezuelan** nationals can travel to Slovenia for up to 90 days within 180 days without a visa.

fff. Citizens of the Special Administrative Regions of the People's Republic of China, namely Hong Kong and Macao, are not required to obtain a visa to enter Slovenia for up to 90 days within 180 days.

ggg. British Overseas Territories Citizens (BOTC): Individuals who are BOTC citizens are exempt from visa requirements to enter Slovenia for up to 90 days within 180 days.

It's important to remember that the requirements for visa exemption, such as the length of stay and the reason for the visit, must be strictly followed. You must apply for the appropriate visa if you intend to visit Slovenia for a duration longer than the allotted period without a visa or for purposes other than those that are authorized.

List of Countries That Are Not Visa Exempt in Slovenia

To ensure a simple and hassle-free trip, travelers from these nations must be aware of the visa requirements.

Visa requirements for entry into Slovenia:

- **Afghanistan**: Before departing for Slovenia, Afghan nationals must obtain a visa. They must submit a visa application at the Slovenian Embassy or Consulate in their home country.

- **Algeria**: Algerian nationals must obtain a visa to enter Slovenia. They must submit a visa application at the Slovenian Embassy or Consulate in their home country.

- **Angola**: Before visiting Slovenia, citizens of Angola must obtain a visa. They must submit a visa application at the Slovenian Embassy or Consulate in their home country.

- **Armenia**: Before departing for Slovenia, Armenian nationals must obtain a visa. They must submit a visa application at the Slovenian Embassy or Consulate in their home country.

- **Azerbaijan**: Before visiting Slovenia, citizens of Azerbaijan must obtain a visa. They must submit a visa application at the Slovenian Embassy or Consulate in their home country.
- **Bahrain**: Bahraini nationals must obtain a visa to enter Slovenia. They must submit a visa application at the Slovenian Embassy or Consulate in their home country.
- **Bangladesh**: Before traveling to Slovenia, residents of Bangladesh must obtain a visa. They must submit a visa application at the Slovenian Embassy or Consulate in their home country.
- **Belarus**: Before visiting Slovenia, citizens of Belarus must obtain a visa. They must submit a visa application at the Slovenian Embassy or Consulate in their home country.
- **Benin**: Before visiting Slovenia, citizens of Benin must obtain a visa. They must submit a visa application at the Slovenian Embassy or Consulate in their home country.
- **Bhutan:** Before visiting Slovenia, citizens of Bhutan must obtain a visa. They must submit a visa

application at the Slovenian Embassy or Consulate in their home country.

- **Bolivia**: Bolivian nationals must obtain a visa to enter Slovenia. They must submit a visa application at the Slovenian Embassy or Consulate in their home country.

- **Botswana:** Before departing for Slovenia, citizens of Botswana must obtain a visa. They must submit a visa application at the Slovenian Embassy or Consulate in their home country.

- **Burkina Faso**: Before visiting Slovenia, citizens of Burkina Faso must obtain a visa. They must submit a visa application at the Slovenian Embassy or Consulate in their home country.

- **Burundi:** Before visiting Slovenia, citizens of Burundi must obtain a visa. They must submit a visa application at the Slovenian Embassy or Consulate in their home country.

- **Cambodia**: Before visiting Slovenia, citizens of Cambodia must obtain a visa. They must submit a visa application at the Slovenian Embassy or Consulate in their home country.

- **Cameroon**: Before visiting Slovenia, citizens of Cameroon must obtain a visa. They must submit a visa application at the Slovenian Embassy or Consulate in their home country.

- **Cape Verde:** Before visiting Slovenia, citizens of Cape Verde must obtain a visa. They must submit a visa application at the Slovenian Embassy or Consulate in their home country.

- **Central African Republic**: Before visiting Slovenia, citizens of the Central African Republic must obtain a visa. They must submit a visa application at the Slovenian Embassy or Consulate in their home country.

- **Chad**: Before visiting Slovenia, citizens of Chad must obtain a visa. They must submit a visa application at the Slovenian Embassy or Consulate in their home country.

- **China**: Before visiting Slovenia, Chinese nationals must obtain a visa. They must submit a visa application at the Slovenian Embassy or Consulate in their home country.

- **Comoros:** Before visiting Slovenia, Comoros nationals must apply for a visa. They must submit a visa application at the Slovenian Embassy or Consulate in their home country.

- **Congo**: Before visiting Slovenia, Congolese nationals must obtain a visa. They must submit a visa application at the Slovenian Embassy or Consulate in their home country.

- **Democratic Republic of the Congo:** Before visiting Slovenia, citizens of the Democratic Republic of the Congo must obtain a visa. They must submit a visa application at the Slovenian Embassy or Consulate in their home country.

- **Cote d'Ivoire**: Before visiting Slovenia, citizens of Cote d'Ivoire must obtain a visa. They must submit a visa application at the Slovenian Embassy or Consulate in their home country.

- **Cuba:** Before visiting Slovenia, citizens of Cuba must obtain a visa. They must submit a visa application at the Slovenian Embassy or Consulate in their home country.

- **Djibouti**: Before visiting Slovenia, citizens of Djibouti must obtain a visa. They must submit a visa application at the Slovenian Embassy or Consulate in their home country.

- **Dominican Republic:** Before visiting Slovenia, Dominican Republic nationals must obtain a visa. They must submit a visa application at the Slovenian Embassy or Consulate in their home country.

- **Ecuador**: Before traveling to Slovenia, Ecuadorian nationals must obtain a visa. They must submit a visa application at the Slovenian Embassy or Consulate in their home country.

- **Egypt**: Before departing for Slovenia, Egyptian nationals must obtain a visa. They must submit a visa application at the Slovenian Embassy or Consulate in their home country.

- **Equatorial Guinea**: Before visiting Slovenia, citizens of Equatorial Guinea must obtain a visa. They must submit a visa application at the Slovenian Embassy or Consulate in their home country.

- **Eritrea**: Eritrean nationals must obtain a visa to enter Slovenia. They must submit a visa application at the Slovenian Embassy or Consulate in their home country.

- **Eswatini:** Eswatini nationals must obtain a visa to enter Slovenia. They must submit a visa application at the Slovenian Embassy or Consulate in their home country.

- **Ethiopia**: Before visiting Slovenia, Ethiopian nationals must obtain a visa. They must submit a visa application at the Slovenian Embassy or Consulate in their home country.
- **Fiji**: Before visiting Slovenia, citizens of Fiji must obtain a visa. They must submit a visa application at the Slovenian Embassy or Consulate in their home country.
- **Gabon**: Before visiting Slovenia, Gabonese nationals must obtain a visa. They must submit a visa application at the Slovenian Embassy or Consulate in their home country.
- **Gambia**: Before visiting Slovenia, citizens of the Gambia must obtain a visa. They must submit a visa application at the Slovenian Embassy or Consulate in their home country.
- **Ghana:** Before traveling to Slovenia, citizens of Ghana must obtain a visa. They must submit a visa application at the Slovenian Embassy or Consulate in their home country.
- **Guinea**: Before visiting Slovenia, citizens of Guinea must obtain a visa. They must submit a visa

application at the Slovenian Embassy or Consulate in their home country.

- **Guinea-Bissau**: Before visiting Slovenia, citizens of Guinea-Bissau must obtain a visa. They must submit a visa application at the Slovenian Embassy or Consulate in their home country.
- **Haiti**: Before visiting Slovenia, citizens of Haiti must obtain a visa. They must submit a visa application at the Slovenian Embassy or Consulate in their home country.
- **India**: Before visiting Slovenia, Indian nationals must obtain a visa. They must submit a visa application at the Slovenian Embassy or Consulate in their home country.
- **Indonesia**: Before visiting Slovenia, citizens of Indonesia must obtain a visa. They must submit a visa application at the Slovenian Embassy or Consulate in their home country.
- **Iran**: Iranian nationals must obtain a visa to enter Slovenia. They must submit a visa application at the Slovenian Embassy or Consulate in their home country.
- **Iraq**: Iraqi nationals must obtain a visa to enter Slovenia. They must submit a visa application at the

Slovenian Embassy or Consulate in their home country.

- **Jamaican** nationals must apply for a visa in advance of visiting Slovenia. They must submit a visa application at the Slovenian Embassy or Consulate in their home country.

- **Jordan**: Before visiting Slovenia, citizens of Jordan must obtain a visa. They must submit a visa application at the Slovenian Embassy or Consulate in their home country.

- **Kazakhstan**: Before visiting Slovenia, citizens of Kazakhstan must obtain a visa. They must submit a visa application at the Slovenian Embassy or Consulate in their home country.

- **Kenya**: Kenyan nationals must obtain a visa to enter Slovenia. They must submit a visa application at the Slovenian Embassy or Consulate in their home country.

- **Kiribati**: Before visiting Slovenia, citizens of Kiribati must obtain a visa. They must submit a visa application at the Slovenian Embassy or Consulate in their home country.

- **Kuwait**: Before traveling to Slovenia, citizens of Kuwait must obtain a visa. They must submit a visa

application at the Slovenian Embassy or Consulate in their home country.

This page was left blank intentionally

Brief History and Culture of Slovenia People

Slovenia is a tiny, alluring nation with a rich history and vibrant culture that is tucked away in the center of Europe. Due to their varied cultural influences, geographical location, and historical experiences, the Slovenian people have developed a distinct identity. In this chapter, I will delve into the fascinating past and present of the Slovenian people, tracing their ancestry from prehistoric times to the present.

Ancient Origins:

The region was inhabited by numerous ancient cultures during the prehistoric era, which is when Slovenia's history began. Archaeological discoveries show proof of human habitation dating back to the Paleolithic era. One of the earliest known inhabitants of the region was a confederation of Indo-European tribes called the Illyrians. The Celts eventually absorbed them after establishing a presence in the area in the 4th century BC.

Roman-era influence

The Slovenian lands then referred to as Pannonia, were significantly impacted by the Roman Empire. Emona (modern-day Ljubljana), the region's capital, was one of the significant settlements built by the Romans. Romanization facilitated the spread of Latin language and culture, which had a long-lasting impact on Slovenians.

The arrival of Slavs and State Formation

The Slavic influence in Slovenia began with the arrival of the Slavic tribes in the sixth century AD. The Slavs brought their culture, language, and traditions with them, laying the groundwork for the growth of Slovenian culture. Slovenia was a part of the Frankish Empire during the Middle Ages and later came under the control of the Holy Roman Empire.

Slovene Enlightenment and Habsburg Rule:

Slovenia came under the long-ruling Habsburg dynasty's rule in the fourteenth century. The Germanization and the spread of Catholicism brought about by the Habsburg era had a profound effect on the Slovenian people. The Slovenian Enlightenment, however, promoted a revival of the language, literature, and cultural identity of Slovenia in the 18th century under the leadership of significant intellectuals like Janez Vajkard Valvasor and Anton Toma Linhart.

Nationwide Awakening and Independence War:

A period of national awakening among the Slovenian people occurred in the 19th century. There was a strong sense of national identity developed in Slovenia as a result of intellectuals, writers, and activists working to preserve and promote their cultural heritage. After the Austro-Hungarian Empire fell at the end of World War I, the Slovenian national movement gained traction in the late 19th and early 20th centuries, culminating in the creation of the State of Slovenes, Croats, and Serbs.

The Independence of Yugoslavia:

The Kingdom of Serbs, Croats, and Slovenes, which later became known as the Kingdom of Yugoslavia, included Slovenia after World War I. Slovenia was occupied by the Axis powers during World War II, and a resistance movement called the Partisans fought to end the occupation. Slovenia joined the Socialist Federal Republic of Yugoslavia as one of its six republics after the war. Slovenia, however, declared its independence in 1991, peacefully breaking away from Yugoslavia, as the desire for independence grew stronger in the late 20th century.

Traditions and cultural heritage:

Slovenia's geographic position at the nexus of various cultures has shaped Slovenian culture, which is a rich tapestry of various influences. The primary language of communication and unifying factor for the Slovenian people is the South Slavic language of Slovenian. The country's distinctive cultural heritage is displayed through traditional folk customs and rituals like the Kurentovanje carnival and Pust celebrations.

Books, music, and the arts

Slovenia has a thriving literary tradition, with well-known writers like France Preeren and Drago Janar adding to its diverse literary landscape. Slovenian folk music, which is characterized by vintage instruments like the accordion and the tamburica, pays homage to the nation's rural past. Joe Plenik and France Miheli are two well-known Slovenian artists who have significantly influenced painting and architecture in the visual arts.

This page was left blank intentionally

7 Notable festivals and cultural events in Slovenia No One Tells You

Although the nation is well known for its breathtaking natural beauty, its extensive cultural heritage is also enthralling. In this chapter, I will examine seven significant festivals and cultural events in Slovenia that, though they may not be well-known, provide both residents and visitors with distinctive and enriching experiences.

1. The Maribor Theatre Festival

It is held each October in Maribor, the second-largest city in Slovenia. This renowned event brings together the best theater companies from around the world and showcases a wide variety of performances, from avant-garde productions to classic plays. Theater enthusiasts should not miss the festival because of its energetic atmosphere and cutting-edge theatrical performances.

2. The Lent Festival

Which takes place every year in Maribor, is one of Slovenia's biggest and oldest summer festivals. The festival, which takes place over two weeks in June, turns the city's streets and public spaces into vibrant stages for performances of music, dance, theater, and visual arts. The region's diverse cultural heritage is reflected in a vibrant variety of performances, exhibitions, and culinary delights that visitors can enjoy.

3. **Piran Musical Evenings**:

The Piran Musical Evenings is a well-known classical music festival that takes place in the summer in the charming coastal town of Piran. This festival, which was founded in 1961, draws musicians and orchestras of renown from around the world to perform in the charming settings of Piran's historic venues. Music lovers will have an unforgettable experience thanks to the town's romantic atmosphere and top-notch music.

4. **Lako's Pivo in Cvetje (Beer and Flowers) Festival**

It brings together music, beer, and flowers in a special way. It takes place in July. This jovial celebration honors the town's brewing heritage and its picturesque landscape covered in vibrant flowers. Visitors to the festival can take in the festive atmosphere while listening to live music performances by well-known Slovenian and international artists.

5. Vilenica International Literary Festival:

The Vilenica International Literary Festival attracts well-known authors, poets, and readers from Slovenia and abroad each September. This esteemed occasion, which offers a venue for literary discussions, readings, and award ceremonies, takes place in the picturesque Karst region. The festival highlights the breadth and depth of contemporary literature while fostering cross-cultural dialogue.

6. The Ana Desetnica Street Theatre Festival

Which takes place in Ljubljana in July, features enthralling street performances that bring the city's streets and squares to life. A variety of performances are presented by international and regional street theater groups, including juggling, mime, puppetry, and acrobatics. Visitors can interact with performances at the festival and get a firsthand look at the magic of street theater thanks to its interactive and open design.

7. Maribor Festival Lent:

An annual multi-genre festival called Festival Lent takes place in Maribor and draws a large number of tourists. This two-week-long cultural extravaganza offers a varied program of performances in the performing arts, visual arts, culinary arts, and dance. Festival Lent promotes a vibrant and welcoming cultural environment by providing something for everyone, from outdoor concerts and theatrical productions to art exhibitions and workshops.

Program for Visa Waiver

An important initiative to ease international travel and advance tourism between nations is the Program for Visa Waiver. Through this program, specific nations enter into bilateral agreements that grant their citizens the ability to travel without a visa for a predetermined amount of time. In this chapter, I will explains how the Program for Visa Waiver enhances travel and tourism while ensuring security and cooperation between participating countries. It also examines the advantages, conditions, and implications of the program.

Through the Program for Visa Waiver, nationals of participating nations can visit certain places without getting a conventional visa. It simplifies the entry procedure, lowering administrative burdens and improving the effectiveness of global travel. This program's main goals are to boost tourism, encourage cross-cultural exchange, and improve international relations while upholding strict security measures.

Benefits of the Visa Waiver Program

- **Tourism Industry Boo**st: The Program for Visa Waiver has a major positive impact on the tourism sectors of participating nations. The removal of the visa requirement will encourage more visitors, which will increase tourist arrivals, increase spending on lodging, dining, and local attractions, and have a positive effect on the economy as a whole.

- **The promotion** of cultural exchange and the facilitation of interpersonal relationships are two benefits of visa exemptions. Travelers can get a firsthand look at the local customs, traditions, and way of life, which promotes international understanding and appreciation. This encourages intercultural communication and fortifies interpersonal bonds, ultimately fostering peace and cooperation on a global scale.

- **Enhanced Business Opportunities**: The program's visa-free travel policy fosters cooperative business environments. Without the hassle of applying for a visa, business owners, investors, and professionals can look into potential partnerships, go to conferences and trade shows, and conduct international business. This encourages global cooperation and helps the economy grow.

- Travel procedures are made simpler thanks to the Program for Visa Waiver, which also cuts down on paperwork and processing times. By passing the protracted visa application procedure, travelers can plan their trips more quickly and easily. This efficient method encourages impulsive travel decisions and saves time and money.

- **Reciprocity and diplomatic ties**: The foundation of many visa waiver programs is the idea of reciprocity, wherein the citizens of the participating nations are granted the same rights to travel without a visa. Promoting equality and respect for one another improves diplomatic ties and lays the groundwork for future collaboration in a variety of areas.

Conditions and Requirements:

Although the Program for Visa Waiver has many advantages, it is crucial to uphold strict security measures and entry requirements. Some typical prerequisites and conditions are as follows:

- **To be eligible for visa-free travel, people must have a valid electronic travel authorization (ETA)** that is specific to the participating country. By providing the necessary personal and travel information during an online application process, this authorization is typically obtained.

- **Purpose and Length of Stay:** Programs that waive visa requirements usually specify the reason for and length of permitted stays. Travelers are required to abide by the established rules and may also be subject to additional limitations, such as prohibitions on employment or study while visiting.

- **Valid Passport:** A valid passport is a prerequisite for travel that doesn't require a visa. The passport must be valid for at least the length of the intended stay, which is typically six months. Participants' passport holders must make sure their travel documents meet the requirements for validity.

- **Security Checks**: Although visa waivers encourage easy travel, security checks are still required. For the safety and integrity of the visa waiver program, travelers may still be subject to security checks, such as biometric scans, background checks, and immigration inspections.

- **Compliance with Laws and Regulations**: To travel without a visa, travelers must follow the laws and regulations of the destination country. If local laws are broken, there may be repercussions, such as deportation and travel bans, which could jeopardize future privileges of visa waiver.

This page was left blank intentionally

The Best Time in the Year to Visit Slovenia

Every traveler can find something to enjoy in Slovenia, from the breathtaking alpine landscapes to the quaint coastal towns and energetic cities. To make the most of your trip, you must choose the best time to go, though. This guide will examine Slovenia's various seasons and highlight the ideal times to go based on the climate, events, and outdoor activities to make sure you have an enjoyable and memorable trip.

March through May:

In Slovenia, spring is a wonderful season when nature emerges from its winter hibernation. It is the perfect time of year for nature enthusiasts and photographers because the countryside is transformed by the blooming flowers into a riot of color. The mild to moderately cool temperatures start to warm up, making outdoor activities comfortable. You can go on a hike through the picturesque Julian Alps in the spring, explore the magnificent Triglav National Park, or go to Lake Bled. Additionally, the Easter celebrations and customary carnivals in the coastal towns give your trip a cultural flair.

Summertime (June through August)

Slovenia's busiest travel season is unquestionably the summer because of the country's great weather and abundance of outdoor activities. This time of year is warm, with temperatures ranging from mild to hot. It is ideal for exploring charming cities, unwinding by the Adriatic Sea, and going on exciting adventures. Summertime provides the best weather for outdoor activities like biking, hiking, and water sports. During this time, you must visit the breathtaking Kocjan Caves and the stunning Soa Valley. In addition, the summer offers a variety of cultural festivals where you can enjoy performances in the arts, including the Maribor Theatre Festival and the Ljubljana Summer Festival.

Fall (September through November)

With its colorful foliage and pleasant weather, autumn in Slovenia is a truly magical time of year. A picturesque tapestry of red, orange, and gold covers the countryside, resulting in breathtaking landscapes. Autumn is the perfect time for outdoor activities like hiking and exploring beautiful vineyards and wine regions because the temperatures are pleasantly cool. Numerous food and wine festivals, including the customary wine harvest celebrations and the Chestnut Festival in the charming town of Kofja Loka, are held during the autumn harvest season. It's the ideal time to explore the charming capital city of Ljubljana and the historic town of Ptuj due to the calmer atmosphere and smaller crowds.

December through February is winter.

Slovenia's winters, especially in the alpine areas, are like something out of a fairy tale. The nation becomes a winter wonderland with snow-covered vistas, frozen lakes, and quaint towns. Wintertime temperatures in popular resorts like Kranjska Gora and Vogel range from cool to cold, making skiing, snowboarding, and other winter sports possible. With its frozen surface and snow-covered surroundings, the famous Lake Bled assumes a magical appearance. Christmas markets in Ljubljana and other cities provide a festive ambiance with ethnic foods and handcrafted goods. Winter is also a great time to indulge in spa getaways and wellness pursuits to unwind and revive.

When to Avoid Visiting Slovenia

Slovenia is a year-round vacation spot that has something to offer every traveler because of its breathtaking landscapes, exciting cities, and rich cultural heritage. However, there are times when traveling to Slovenia might not be the best idea due to a variety of reasons like the weather, a lack of attractions, or heavy tourist traffic. To give you the best experience possible, we will go over the times of year you might want to think twice about visiting Slovenia in this extensive guide.

Winter Break:

Although Slovenia's alpine regions are renowned for their beautiful winter scenery and fantastic skiing, the winter break, especially around Christmas and New Year, can be very busy. Overcrowding at well-known tourist locations like Lake Bled and ski resorts can lead to longer lines, more expensive lodging, and limited availability. Avoid going during the busiest winter holiday season if you want a quieter, more laid-back experience.

Summer is Slovenia's busiest travel season when warm temperatures and a wide range of outdoor activities draw tourists. But this popularity also brings with it more people and more expensive offerings. Particularly in July and August, the busiest tourist locations, like Lake Bled, Ljubljana, and coastal towns like Piran, can become crowded. Consider going to Slovenia in the shoulder seasons of spring or autumn if you want to avoid the tourist crowds and have a more relaxing time.

Easter Holidays:

Easter is a significant religious holiday in Slovenia, and many citizens use this period to travel domestically or to see loved ones. Therefore, restaurants, museums, and tourist attractions may operate with shortened hours or with fewer services during this time. On top of that, Easter Sunday and Easter Monday might be closed for some businesses and stores. Plan your trip outside of the Easter holiday period if you prefer to have access to the full range of amenities and attractions.

Public Holidays and National Holidays:

Throughout the year, Slovenia observes several public holidays and national holidays. These include Statehood Day (June 25), France Preeren Day (February 8), Slovenia's National Day (June 25), and others. Preeren Day honors Slovenia's greatest poet. Even though these holidays can provide interesting cultural experiences, they can also lead to business closures, constrained public transportation, and overcrowded tourist attractions. It is advised that you review the list of Slovenian public holidays and adjust your travel schedule accordingly.

November and February:

In Slovenia, these two months are regarded as off-peak. With colder temperatures and greater chances of rain and snowfall, the weather during these months can be erratic. Due to weather, some tourist attractions, particularly those that are outdoors or at higher altitudes, may be closed or have restricted access. Plan your trip during more favored seasons if you prefer to take in Slovenia's natural beauty and participate in outdoor activities.

Major Festivals and Events:

While Slovenia's festivals and events can be the highlight of your trip, they can also lead to congested streets and a shortage of lodging. Numerous people attend events like the Pivo in Cvetje Festival in Lako, the Maribor Theatre Festival, and the Ljubljana Summer Festival. It's a good idea to look at the event calendar and make travel arrangements if you'd prefer a quieter experience or have specific attractions in mind.

When is the Cheapest Time to Visit Slovenia?

Travelers will have a memorable experience in Slovenia thanks to its picturesque landscapes, quaint towns, and rich cultural heritage. If you're considering visiting this lovely nation, you might be curious to know when it's least expensive. By planning your trip appropriately, you can travel on a tighter budget, stay in more affordable lodgings, and benefit from lower rates. In this chapter, I will examine the various elements that affect the price of traveling to Slovenia and will highlight the times of the year when you can get the best offers and most affordable options.

Off-peak Seasons: Traveling to Slovenia in the off-peak seasons is one of the best ways to reduce the cost of your trip. These are the times of the year when there is a decline in tourist activity and a consequent decrease in the cost of lodging, travel, and attractions. Slovenia's shoulder seasons are primarily from March to May in the spring and from September to November in the fall, excluding major holidays and events. In addition to finding cheaper hotel rates during these times, you'll also find less crowding at popular attractions and get to experience more real travel.

Winter in Slovenia, especially in the alpine regions, offers breathtaking scenery and opportunities for winter sports (excluding major holidays). You can find more affordable rates, though, if you schedule your trip outside of the busiest Christmas and New Year holiday periods. Ski resorts, such as Kranjska Gora and Vogel, provide discounted lodging and lift tickets during off-peak times. Enjoy the winter wonderland, go skiing or snowboarding, and benefit from the less-crowded slopes and quieter terrain.

Early Spring and Late Autumn: If you want to enjoy Slovenia's scenic landscapes while keeping costs down, think about traveling there in the early spring or late autumn. The countryside awakens in the early spring (March to April) with blooming flowers and lush greenery. It's a great time to go hiking, explore parks like Triglav, and take in the rebirth of nature. Similar to late summer, late autumn (October to November) offers the opportunity to take in the breathtaking fall foliage, visit vineyards during the harvest, and save money on lodging.

Weekdays and Non-Holiday Times: If you can, try to visit Slovenia between Monday and Thursday during the week to save money. Due to the lower occupancy during the weekdays, many hotels and places to stay offer discounted rates. Additionally, avoid traveling during Slovenian public holidays as these times are generally more expensive for lodging and travel. You can take advantage of less expensive rates and fewer crowds by scheduling your trip for off-peak times and staying on a weekday.

Booking Far Ahead or at the Last Minute: Scheduling your trip far in advance or taking advantage of last-minute discounts are additional methods for locating less expensive options. You can frequently get better deals and benefit from early bird discounts by making your travel arrangements for your flights and lodging several months in advance. However, if you can be flexible with your travel dates, you can search for last-minute offers and discounts. Nearer to the travel dates, many travel companies and online booking services offer discounted rates for unsold inventory.

Think About Alternative Accommodation Options: In addition to picking the best time to travel, thinking about alternative accommodations can help you save money. Although Slovenia has several inexpensive lodging options, hotels can be more expensive, especially during the busiest times of the year. Think about staying in guesthouses, hostels, or apartments, which are frequently more affordable. Along with offering more affordable lodging options, exploring smaller towns and villages outside of popular tourist destinations can let you experience Slovenia's authentic local culture.

Use Public Transportation: Slovenia has a well-connected and effective public transportation system, which includes trains and buses and can be a convenient way to see the country at a reasonable price. To get around, think about using public transportation rather than hiring a car or calling a cab. This not only reduces the cost of transportation but also does away with the need for parking fees and fuel expenditures. Public transportation makes for an easy and cost-effective means of transportation to most major cities and tourist destinations in Slovenia.

Best Time to Visit for Different Travelers

Every kind of traveler can enjoy a variety of experiences in Slovenia, a hidden gem in the middle of Europe. Slovenia has something to offer all year long, from its breathtaking alpine landscapes and quaint coastal towns to vibrant cities and rich cultural heritage. The ideal time to visit, however, can vary based on personal preferences, interests, and travel habits. In this chapter, I will examine the ideal times to visit Slovenia for various traveler types, ensuring that you have a memorable and customized experience.

Nature Lovers: The best times to visit Slovenia are in the spring (March to May) and fall (September to November) if you enjoy the outdoors. These times of year feature pleasant weather and vibrantly colored landscapes. Spring is the best season for hiking, exploring national parks like

Triglav, and taking in the breathtaking alpine scenery because it brings blooming flowers, lush greenery, and cascading waterfalls. In contrast, autumn brings beautiful fall foliage, celebrations of the wine harvest, and a calmer atmosphere for hiking, biking, and exploring the picturesque countryside.

Adventure Seekers: If you're looking for heart-pounding activities, the summer (June to August) is the best time to visit Slovenia. The warm temperatures and longer daylight hours make the environment perfect for a variety of outdoor activities. You can try your hand at canyoning in the breathtaking gorges, go white-water rafting on the emerald Soa River, or paraglide over the Julian Alps. Additionally, the summer months are ideal for water sports on Lake Bled or the Adriatic Sea, cycling through picturesque landscapes, and hiking in the Julian Alps.

Cultural Enthusiasts: The best time to visit Slovenia is during the summer, when several cultural festivals and events are held, allowing visitors to fully immerse themselves in the country's rich cultural heritage. The Ljubljana Summer Festival, which runs from June to

September, features an exciting lineup of musical, theatrical, dance, and visual arts performances. The best of Slovenian theater is presented at the Maribor Theatre Festival, which takes place in October. You can also get a taste of the regional music scene at several music festivals, like the Maribor Lent Festival and the Ljubljana Trnfest.

City explorers: The shoulder seasons of spring and autumn are the best times to visit if you're attracted to the charm and history of Slovenia's cities. The capital city of Ljubljana is a delight to explore during these times thanks to the pleasant weather, reduced crowds, and abundance of outdoor cafes and eateries. In the off-peak months, you can avoid the summertime crowds and take in the historic coastal town of Piran's winding streets, charming squares, and picturesque sea views. A more relaxed and immersive experience is made possible by the quieter environment.

Winter Enthusiasts: The best time to visit Slovenia is during the winter months (December to February), which are ideal for those who enjoy snowy landscapes and winter sports. The country's alpine regions, such as Kranjska Gora and Vogel, provide fantastic opportunities for skiing, snowboarding, and cross-country skiing. With its frozen surface and snow-covered surroundings, Lake Bled assumes a magical appearance. Mulled wine, traditional foods, and handcrafted goods are available at Christmas markets in Ljubljana and other cities, creating a festive atmosphere.

Wine and food connoisseurs: The autumn (September to November) is the best time to visit Slovenia because it is when the grape harvest takes place. You can tour the Tajerska, Primorska, and Posavje wine regions, take part in wine-growing and grape-picking activities, and savor delectable cuisine. Traditional food festivals that feature regional specialties like potica (nut roll), truklji (rolled dumplings), and morn (fluffy pancake dessert) are held in the autumn.

Best Time to Visit for Honeymoon

A honeymoon is a special occasion where newlyweds can cherish their union and celebrate their love. To ensure a romantic and unforgettable experience, it is essential to pick the ideal location and time for your honeymoon. You'll be happy to learn that Slovenia, an enchanting country, offers a variety of romantic settings and experiences all year long if you're thinking about making Slovenia your honeymoon destination. In this chapter, I will discuss the ideal time to travel to Slovenia for a honeymoon, taking into account elements like the weather, tourist density, and romantic activities.

Spring (March to May): As Slovenia emerges from its winter hibernation, spring is a romantic time to travel there for a honeymoon. The mild weather, along with the blooming flowers, the lush greenery, and the cascading waterfalls, make for a romantic backdrop. You can stroll hand in hand along the picturesque shores of Lake Bled, take a leisurely boat ride on Lake Bohinj, or explore the charming capital city of Ljubljana. Visits to Slovenia's enthralling caves, like Postojna Cave or Kocjan Caves, where you can be in awe of the magnificent underground formations and have an unforgettable underground experience, are also possible in the spring.

Summer (June to August): The warm, sunny summer months are a popular time to visit Slovenia because they are ideal for a romantic honeymoon. There is plenty of time to explore the nation's natural wonders and engage in outdoor activities thanks to the long daylight hours. You can go on a passionate hike through the Julian Alps, see the breathtaking Vintgar Gorge, or cool off in Lake Bled's pristine waters. The Slovenian coast offers a romantic seaside getaway with charming towns like Piran and Portoro, complete with romantic strolls along promenades at dusk and candlelit dinners overlooking the Adriatic Sea.

Autumn (September to November): The romantic atmosphere and vibrant colors of Slovenia's autumn season make it a great choice for a honeymoon. The scenery changes into a tapestry of golden tones, providing an incredible backdrop for leisurely walks and scenic drives.

You can visit charming wine regions like Maribor's or the Vipava Valley's vineyards, where you can partake in wine tastings and enjoy the flavors of the harvest season. With the vibrant fall foliage all around it, the picturesque Lake Bled appears to be floating in a magical world. Visit the charming town of Ptuj in the autumn, which is known for its romantic ambiance and medieval castle.

Winter (December to February): Slovenia provides a romantic setting for couples who value a winter wonderland and cozy experiences. When the landscapes are covered in snow, it creates a magical setting ideal for curling up by the fireplace and taking in the beauty. Visit quaint alpine communities like Kranjska Gora or Bled to engage in winter activities like skiing, snowboarding, or ice skating. Christmas markets in Ljubljana and other cities provide a romantic atmosphere with twinkling lights, mulled wine, and handcrafted gifts, adding a touch of magic to the festive season.

Special Occasions and Festivals: If you're basing your honeymoon plans on a holiday or festival, Slovenia hosts several activities that can heighten the romance of your trip.

For instance, the Ljubljana Summer Festival, which runs from June to September, features a varied schedule of musical, theatrical, and dance performances that offer a culturally and romantically enriching experience. Theater lovers can enjoy a memorable date night at the Maribor Theatre Festival, which takes place in October and features the best of Slovenian theater. A festive and enchanting atmosphere is also created by the various Christmas and New Year's Eve celebrations that take place in Slovenia's cities.

The Best Time to Visit Slovenia for Amazing Weather Condition

Slovenia is a country with a variety of landscapes and climates, providing travelers with a wide range of experiences all year long. It is essential to take the weather into account when making travel plans to Slovenia if you want to have a relaxing and enjoyable stay. The best time to visit Slovenia for wonderful weather is crucial whether you're looking for hot, sunny days or a winter wonderland. In this chapter, I will cover every season as well as the best times to visit Slovenia to take advantage of its spectacular weather.

Spring (March to May):

After a long winter, spring in Slovenia is a time of rebirth for the natural world. As the weather gradually gets warmer, it's a great time to travel the nation. These are the main characteristics of Slovenia's springtime climate:

a. **Mild weather:** Slovenia experiences an average temperature of 4°C to 12°C (39°F to 54°F) in March and 9°C to 19°C (48°F to 66°F) in May. In general, the weather is pleasant and conducive to outdoor activities.

b. **Blooming Nature**: In the spring, Slovenia's landscapes take on the appearance of a vibrant tapestry. As the seasons change, trees and flowers bloom and the countryside turns a vibrant shade of green. For those who appreciate the beauty of nature, now is the perfect time to visit Slovenia's national parks, including Triglav National Park and the breathtaking Julian Alps.

c. **Occasional Rainfall**: Spring is a season with pleasant weather, but it is also one with sporadic rainfall. During your visit, be ready for a few showers, and it's a good idea to bring an umbrella or rain jacket.

d. **Fewer Tourists:** Spring in Slovenia is regarded as a shoulder season, which means fewer visitors than during the busiest summer months. This enables you to enjoy a more intimate experience while exploring well-known attractions in peace.

Summer (June to August):

Summer is Slovenia's busiest travel season, with warm, sunny days ideal for outdoor activities. What to anticipate over the summer is as follows:?

a. In the summer, Slovenia averages temperatures between 59 and 77 degrees Fahrenheit (15 to 25 degrees Celsius). Highs of 30°C (86°F) or more are occasionally recorded in July and August, particularly in coastal regions.

b. **Lengthier Days**: Slovenian summers feature lengthy days with up to 15 hours of daylight. This gives plenty of time for outdoor exploration and recreation.

c. **Dynamic Coastal Climate**: The coastal region of Slovenia, which includes cities like Piran and Portoro, experiences a Mediterranean climate in the summer. The slight increase in temperature is accompanied by cooling coastal breezes.

d. **Peak Travel Season**: The summer is Slovenia's busiest season, with more visitors and more expensive lodging. To guarantee availability, it's a good idea to reserve your lodging and popular attractions in advance.

e. **Summertime** in Slovenia is the time for a lot of outdoor festivals and cultural events. You'll have the chance to fully immerse yourself in the vibrant cultural scene of the nation, from music festivals to art exhibitions.

Autumn (September to November):

Slovenia's autumn is a season of breathtaking hues and more comfortable temperatures. What to anticipate during this lovely season is as follows:

a. **Comfortable Temperatures:** September has warm, summer-like temperatures between 15°C and 25°C (59°F and 77°F). Temperatures gradually decrease throughout the season, averaging 5° to 15°C (41° to 59°F) in November.

b. **Stunning Fall Colors**: Slovenia is famous for its stunning fall colors. Particularly in national parks like Triglav National Park and the Logar Valley, the landscapes change into a kaleidoscope of vivid reds, oranges, and yellows.

Harvest festivals are held in Slovenia during the autumn when the country is amid a rich tradition of wine-making and other agricultural pursuits. During this time, a variety of harvest festivals are held, providing an opportunity to sample regional cuisine and take part in customary festivities.

d. **Less Tourist Traffic:** Similar to spring, autumn is regarded as a shoulder season, with less traveler traffic than during the summer. This offers a chance to take in Slovenia's attractions and natural beauty in a more serene environment.

Winter (December to February):

Slovenia's winters are particularly magical for fans of winter sports and joyous celebrations. What to anticipate in the winter is as follows:

a. **Cold Temperatures:** Depending on the region, Slovenian winter temperatures can vary greatly. While the alpine regions can experience below-freezing temperatures, the lowlands experience temperatures between -2°C and 5°C (28°F and 41°F). Snowboarding and skiing are best enjoyed in the Julian Alps, which receives a lot of snowfall.

b. **Winter Sports:** Slovenia has world-class winter sports facilities at its ski resorts, including Kranjska Gora, Vogel, and Rogla. You can engage in snow-related activities such as cross-country skiing, skiing, and snowboarding. Winter adventures have a beautiful backdrop thanks to the snowy landscapes.

c. **Festive Atmosphere**: Slovenians love to celebrate and shop at festive markets during the winter. Charming Christmas markets are held in cities like Ljubljana, Maribor, and Bled where you can browse for one-of-a-kind gifts, eat local fare, and get into the holiday spirit.

d. **Thermal Spas**: Slovenia is renowned for its thermal spas, which make for the ideal wintertime retreat. Many spa resorts offer wellness services and amenities, and soaking in warm thermal waters is a soothing experience.

This page was left blank intentionally

When is the Best Time to go Mountaineering in Slovenia?

Slovenia offers a diverse landscape that includes imposing mountains and breathtaking alpine scenery, making it a haven for outdoor enthusiasts. Slovenia is a popular destination for adventurers from all over the world to go mountaineering. To ensure a safe and enjoyable experience, you should carefully plan your mountaineering trip, taking into account the weather and the best time. We will examine the various seasons and highlight the ideal time to go mountaineering in Slovenia in this thorough guide.

Spring (March to May):

As the snow starts to melt and nature awakens from its winter slumber, spring in Slovenia is a time of transition. What you should know before going mountaineering in Slovenia in the spring is as follows:

a. Early spring can have unpredictable weather because the higher mountain regions are still covered in snow. The trails become easier to access as the season goes on thanks to rising temperatures and snowmelt. However, during this time, be prepared for sporadic rainfall and swift weather changes.

b. **Fewer People:** Compared to the busiest summer months, spring is thought of as a shoulder season for mountaineering in Slovenia. This offers the chance for a more tranquil mountaineering experience.

c. **Alpine Flowers**: Seeing the alpine flowers bloom in the spring is one of the highlights of mountaineering. Your mountaineering adventures will take place against a picturesque backdrop of vibrantly blooming meadows.

d. **Snowy Peaks**: Some of the higher peaks may still have a substantial amount of snow on them in the early spring. You can take on more difficult routes that require navigating snowy terrain if you're an experienced mountaineer and have the necessary equipment.

Slovenian mountaineering is most popular during the summer (June to August) when conditions are generally good and the trails are easier to access. What to anticipate over the summer is as follows:

a. **Weather:** Summertime in Slovenia is warm and sunny, with lower elevations experiencing temperatures between 15°C and 25°C (59°F and 77°F). However, temperatures can drop and weather conditions can quickly change as you climb to higher altitudes. It's crucial to carry the proper equipment and be ready for unforeseen weather changes.

b. **Longer Days:** With longer daylight hours during the summer, you'll have more time to explore and scale Slovenia's mountain peaks. To make the most of the daylight, it is advised to begin your mountaineering expeditions early in the day.

c. **Clear Trails:** In the summer, snow and ice have melted from the mountain trails, making travel safer. Mountaineers can stay and get refreshments at the mountain huts and shelters that are open along the routes.

d. **Popular Routes**: The number of mountaineers increases during the summer, especially on well-traveled routes like the one to Slovenia's highest peak, Triglav. Consider exploring lesser-known peaks and trails in the Julian Alps and other mountain ranges if you want a more sedate experience.

e. **Alpine Lakes**: Lake Bled and Lake Bohinj are just a couple of the breathtaking alpine lakes Slovenia is known for. A further element of beauty can be added to your mountaineering trip if you include visits to these lakes.

Autumn (September to November):

Slovenia experiences cooler temperatures and vibrant foliage during the autumn, providing an alluring setting for mountaineering excursions. What you should know about mountaineering in Slovenia in the fall is as follows:

a. **Climate:** Autumn in Slovenia is characterized by cooler temperatures, which in the lower regions range from 5°C to

15°C (41°F to 59°F). Lower temperatures and colder conditions are experienced at higher altitudes as the season goes on. It's crucial to bring the right clothing and equipment on your mountaineering expeditions to stay warm.

b. **Fall Foliage:** Autumn is a magical season in Slovenia when the landscapes take on a spectrum of vivid hues. Red, orange, and gold hues adorn the forests and valleys, making for an exquisite backdrop for your mountaineering expeditions.

c. **Quieter Trails:** Similar to spring, Slovenian mountaineers consider autumn to be a shoulder season. You can experience the trails in greater calmness and peace as the number of tourists and mountaineers declines.

d. **Unpredictable Weather**: The autumn weather in the mountains can change quickly in temperature and may include rain or snow. It's crucial to follow weather updates and be ready for a range of circumstances.

Winter (December to February):

For those who are prepared for colder temperatures and snowy conditions, winter in Slovenia offers a unique mountaineering experience. What you should know about winter mountaineering in Slovenia is as follows:

a. **Weather**: Slovenia experiences cold winters, especially in the higher mountainous areas. Below-freezing temperatures are possible, and snowfall is frequent. To navigate the snowy terrain safely, you must have the necessary mountaineering gear and skills.

b. A breathtaking experience can be had while mountaineering in Slovenia during the winter. For intrepid mountaineers, the snow-covered landscapes, frozen waterfalls, and gleaming peaks create a magical winter wonderland.

c. Slovenia is well known for its ski mountaineering opportunities. If you're an accomplished skier and mountaineer, you can combine the two sports to explore the mountains in the winter. Ski mountaineering enables you to reach inaccessible locations and experience the exhilaration of descending through virgin powder.

d. **Shorter Days**: Slovenian winter days are shorter and have fewer daylight hours. To make the most of your time on the trails, it's critical to plan your mountaineering trips appropriately and leave early.

e. **Safety Considerations**: Winter mountaineering requires advanced skills and avalanche safety knowledge. To ensure your safety during winter expeditions, it is advised to hire a licensed guide or sign up for a scheduled mountaineering tour.

This page was left blank intentionally

When is the Best Time to go Water Sport in Slovenia?

Despite being a landlocked nation, Slovenia is home to numerous beautiful lakes, rivers, and waterways that offer fantastic opportunities for water sports enthusiasts. In Slovenia's clear waters, you can go swimming, rafting, kayaking, and paddle boarding, among other activities. The ideal time to engage in water sports, however, depends on several variables, including the weather, the state of the water, and individual preferences. In this chapter, I will examine the various seasons and highlight the ideal times to engage in water sports in Slovenia.

Spring (March to May):

As nature emerges from its winter hibernation, spring in Slovenia is a time of transition. What you should know about participating in water sports in Slovenia during the spring is as follows:

a. **Weather:** Springtime brings a gradual rise in temperature and a mellower atmosphere. Although temperatures can still be chilly in the early spring, by May they can rise to between 15°C and 20°C (59°F and 68°F). It's important to remember that the water might still be chilly, so wearing the proper wetsuits or safety equipment is advised.

b. **Snowmelt and Water Levels:** As the snow in the mountains melts in the spring, rivers and lakes fill up with more water. Water sports like kayaking and rafting are perfect now because the rivers have exciting rapids and faster currents. However, it's crucial to use caution and take into account your level of expertise before partaking in more difficult water activities.

c. **Emerging Nature**: With its vivid colors and flowering plants, spring is one of Slovenia's most visually stunning seasons. While participating in their favorite activities, water sports enthusiasts can take in the scenic beauty of the surrounding landscapes.

d. **Less Tourist Traffic**: Spring in Slovenia is regarded as a shoulder season for water sports, which means there are fewer visitors than during the busiest summer months. This makes traveling on lakes and rivers more tranquil.

Summer (June to August):

Due to the warm weather and more comfortable water temperatures, summer is the most popular time of year for water sports in Slovenia. What to anticipate over the summer is as follows:

a. The summer months in Slovenia are warm and sunny, with temperatures between 20°C and 30°C (68°F and 86°F). Lakes and rivers warm up to a pleasant temperature, which is perfect for water sports like kayaking and paddleboarding.

b. **Well-liked Water Sports**: Summer in Slovenia is the ideal time for a variety of water sports due to the pleasant weather and warm water temperatures. On the picturesque lakes and rivers of the nation, you can engage in activities like canoeing, kayaking, paddleboarding, swimming, and even sailing whether you're a novice or an experienced enthusiast.

Longer Days: Slovenian summers offer plenty of daylight hours for water sports. Long after sunset, you can continue having fun on the water and taking in the splendor of the surroundings.

d. **Festive Atmosphere**: Slovenia's summer is a lively time of year with lots of festivals, events, and beach parties held close to the lakes and rivers. Along with participating in water sports, you can enjoy the vibrant atmosphere and cultural experiences.

Autumn (September to November):

For lovers of water sports who prefer a more tranquil experience, Slovenia's autumn is the perfect time to visit due to its cooler temperatures and calmer atmosphere. What you should know about water sports in Slovenia in the fall is as follows:

a. **Slovenia's autumn** weather is milder than summer, with temperatures between 15°C and 25°C (59°F and 77°F). Water activities are comfortable because of the relatively warm water temperatures. Though temperatures begin to fall as the season goes on, so it's best to check the weather reports and make your water sports plans in accordance.

b. **Autumn Foliage**: Slovenia's landscapes are adorned in vibrant colors during the autumn, making it an especially beautiful time of year. When you participate in water sports during this time, you can admire the surrounding natural beauty as you float through the water.

c. **Quieter Ambiance:** Autumn is regarded as a shoulder season for water sports, which means that there are fewer visitors and crowds than during the busiest summer months. This offers the chance for a more relaxing and peaceful experience on the rivers and lakes.

d. **Late-season activities**: The autumn is an excellent time to try stand-up paddle boarding (SUP) or canoeing on Slovenia's lakes' calm waters. Water sports enthusiasts can relax in the serene environment and beautiful surroundings.

Winter (December to February):

Slovenia experiences colder temperatures and frozen landscapes during the winter, which makes it less conducive to most water sports. For those who are up for the challenge, there are still chances for uncommon experiences. What you should know about wintertime water sports in Slovenia is as follows:

a. **Ice Skating and Ice Fishing**: In Slovenia, some lakes and rivers freeze over during the winter, providing ideal ice skating and ice fishing conditions. Before performing these activities, it is crucial to make sure the ice is secure and thick enough.

b. **Winter Kayaking**: In Slovenia's rivers, skilled and well-equipped kayakers can experience the exhilaration of winter kayaking. Due to the chilly water temperatures and potentially hazardous conditions, this calls for advanced skills and proper safety measures.

c. **Indoor Water Activities**: Slovenia's indoor water parks offer a variety of activities like swimming, water slides, and water-based fitness classes. If you still yearn for water sports during the winter, you can go there.

This page was left blank intentionally

5 Strategies You Need to Know to Become Good Swimmer

Swimming is a well-liked, enjoyable activity that has many positive health effects. Some specific strategies and techniques can help you become a good swimmer, regardless of whether you're a beginner learning to swim or hoping to improve your swimming abilities. This extensive manual will go over five key techniques that you must master to become a proficient swimmer.

Learn Correct Technique: Developing a good swimming technique requires both learning and practicing it. In particular, pay attention to the following:

a. **Body Position**: Keep your body horizontal in the water, with your head perpendicular to your spine. You can navigate the water more effectively as a result of less drag.

b. **Breathing:** Develop the rhythmic breathing technique, which involves inhaling while swimming with your head turned to the side and exhaling underwater. To increase balance and symmetry, practice bilateral breathing, which involves breathing from both sides.

c. **Arm Stroke**: To develop a powerful and effective arm stroke, reach forward, dip your fingertips into the water first, pull back, and extend your arm fully at the end of the stroke. Be sure to keep your motion smooth and constant.

d. **Leg Kick**: Work on a steady and propulsion leg kick while maintaining straight legs and pointed toes. The kick should complement the arm stroke and should originate from the hips rather than the knees.

e. **Body Rotation:** Make sure your swimming stroke includes body rotation. Turn your body to the side as you pull with one arm, allowing your other arm to extend forward.

Build your stamina and strength because swimming calls for both. Build muscular strength by including strength-training exercises in your routine, focusing on the shoulders, arms, core, and legs. Exercises like lunges, squats, planks, push-ups, and pull-ups can help you improve your swimming technique. To develop endurance, gradually increase your swimming distance and time. Include interval training, where you alternate between quick and slow laps, to improve your stamina and speed.

Concentrate on Breathing Techniques: Keeping a consistent swimming rhythm requires effective breathing. By fully exhaling underwater and inhaling during the appropriate part of your stroke, you can practice controlled breathing. To avoid holding your breath, practice your breathing rhythm and timing. Use swimming aids, such as snorkels or swim fins, if necessary to help you concentrate on perfecting your breathing technique while putting other aspects of your stroke to the side.

Seek Professional Instruction: If you want to improve your swimming technique, think about getting professional instruction. Enroll in swimming lessons or join a club where professional instructors can offer direction, correct any issues with your stroke, and provide individualized feedback. They can provide you with advanced training, assist you in setting goals, and develop structured training schedules that are suited to your abilities and goals.

Consistent practice is essential to improving as a swimmer. You can improve your technique, increase your endurance, and create muscle memory by practicing frequently. Swim sessions should be regular, with frequency and length being gradually increased as you advance. Being able to swim is a skill that requires time and practice, so have patience with yourself. Set attainable objectives, acknowledge your progress, and take pleasure in learning to swim well.

In addition to these tips, always put safety first when swimming. Always be mindful of your surroundings, swim in designated areas where lifeguards are on duty, and adhere to the correct water safety procedures.

How to Stay Safe in Slovenia

Slovenia is a stunning and secure destination with charming cities, warm people, and breathtaking natural scenery. However, just as with any other travel destination, it's crucial to put your safety first and take the appropriate safety measures to guarantee a hassle-free and secure trip. We will examine various pointers and advice on how to stay safe in Slovenia in this thorough guide.

Research and planning: Before going to Slovenia, learn as much as you can about the nation, its people, traditions, and laws. Learn about the areas you intend to visit, as well as the local emergency services, transportation options, and consulates or embassies that are close by.

Obtain thorough travel insurance that includes coverage for medical emergencies, trip cancellation or interruption, and personal effects. Make sure your policy covers any planned activities, like hiking or water sports, and that it is valid for the entire time you will be in Slovenia.

Keep Up: Keep abreast of Slovenia's most recent travel warnings and security updates. To receive critical alerts or notifications in the event of emergencies or changes to the security situation, register with the Slovenian embassy or consulate of your nation.

Personal Safety:

a. Protect Your Property: Always keep your items, such as your wallet, passport, and electronic devices, secure. Keep valuables in hotel safes or lockers, and only bring a small amount of cash with you.

b. **Pickpocketing**: Be mindful of your surroundings and use caution in congested areas, popular destinations, and on public transportation. Keep your pockets and bags closed, and stay away from flashing large amounts of cash or valuables in public.

c. **Save the local emergency contact numbers** for the police (113), ambulance (112), and the fire department (112) in your phone. Call the appropriate number in an emergency and be sure to give the operator precise details about your location and the emergency.

d. **Safety Tips for Solo Travelers**: If you're traveling alone, let someone you trust know your itinerary and lodging information and check in with them frequently. Avoid going for a late-night stroll alone in isolated or dimly lit areas, and think about using a reliable transportation service.

Transportation Security:

a. Driving: If you intend to drive in Slovenia, get to know the country's traffic laws. Always keep your driver's license, registration, and insurance documents on you. Utilize seatbelts, obey posted speed limits, and exercise caution when operating a vehicle on mountain roads.

Slovenia has a dependable and effective public transportation system, which includes buses and trains. Be cautious with your belongings, especially in crowded places, and stay away from nighttime solo travel. For safe transportation, use reputable ride-sharing apps or authorized taxi services.

Outdoor Safety: The stunning scenery of Slovenia provides a wealth of opportunities for outdoor pursuits like hiking, skiing, and water sports. Make sure you're safe by adhering to these rules:

a. Planning your hiking routes, getting trail maps, and checking the weather are all important. Tell someone where you're going on your hike and when you expect to be back. Wear the proper clothing, including sturdy shoes and layers of clothing, and keep a first aid kit, a map, and a compass in your carry-on along with enough food and water.

b. **Water Activities**: If you intend to partake in water sports, make sure you have the knowledge and experience required. Check the weather and the state of the water, wear the proper safety equipment, such as a life jacket, and adhere to the direction of qualified instructors or guides.

Natural hazards, such as abrupt weather changes, avalanches in mountainous areas during the winter, and strong river currents, should be considered. When traveling to remote or unfamiliar areas, pay attention to warning signs, heed local advice, and use caution.

Health and Medical Care:

a. Modern medical facilities are available in Slovenia, which has a well-developed healthcare system. Make sure you carry any necessary prescriptions or medications and that you have adequate health insurance coverage. In case of any medical emergencies, familiarize yourself with the locations of nearby hospitals or clinics.

b. **Vaccinations**: Before traveling to Slovenia, find out from your doctor which shots are advised. Make sure your routine vaccinations are current, and depending on the length and purpose of your trip, you might want to consider getting additional shots.

Cultural Sensitivity:

Be respectful of Slovenian traditions, customs, and cultural norms. When visiting rural or religious locations, dress appropriately. Learn a few fundamental words and expressions in Slovenian to interact with locals and express respect.

Emergency Planning:

a. **Travel Documents**: Make copies of your travel insurance policy, passport, and other crucial papers. Separately store your hard copies and digital copies.

b. Carry a small emergency kit with the necessities, including a portable phone charger, extra batteries, a whistle, a basic first-aid kit, and a flashlight.

c. **Local Information**: Become acquainted with the closest embassy or consulate of your home nation. Contact them for assistance and direction in the event of any emergencies.

When exploring Slovenia, follow your instincts and exercise caution if something seems off or unsafe. Remove yourself from any threatening or suspicious situations and call the police or other authorities in the area for assistance.

This page was left blank intentionally

Is it Safe in Slovenia at Night?

Slovenia is generally regarded as a safe destination for tourists, even at night and during the evening. Slovenia provides visitors with a comfortable and secure environment thanks to its low crime rates, well-kept cities, and friendly atmosphere. To ensure your safety, it is crucial to always use caution and abide by certain rules. The safety considerations and measures you should take when touring Slovenia at night are covered in this guide.

Slovenia's urban areas, which include Ljubljana, Maribor, and Bled, are renowned for their safety and security. These cities have excellent lighting, and police presence, and are generally safe. Nevertheless, it is still wise to exercise caution and be aware of your surroundings, especially in crowded places or popular tourist destinations.

Keep to Well-Lit Areas: When out at night, stay on well-lit streets and steer clear of dimly lit or deserted areas. Keep to main thoroughfares and densely populated areas where other people are present.

b. **Travel in Groups**: There is safety in numbers, so if at all possible, travel with a friend or in a group. Walking in groups is generally safer, especially when exploring new places.

c. **Protect Your Property:** Always keep your personal property secure, especially in crowded places. Keep expensive items and large amounts of cash hidden from view. Keep your belongings close to your body and use bags with secure closures.

d. **Use Reputable Rideshare Services or Licensed Taxis**: If you need to use transportation late at night, it is advised that you do so with respectable rideshare services or licensed taxis. Refrain from getting in unmarked or unofficial vehicles.

Buses and trains are just two of Slovenia's dependable and well-connected public transportation options. Consider the following when using public transportation at night:

a. **Review Schedules**: To make sure you can get back to your lodging safely, be aware of the last bus and train departure times. Plan your trip and become familiar with the schedules and routes.

b. **Busy Stations:** Try to wait in a well-lit, populated area if you have to wait at a bus or train station at night. Be watchful and keep an eye on your possessions.

c. **Sit Close to the Driver or Conductor**: When taking public transportation, try to sit close to the driver or conductor. This may increase security and serve to ward off potential problems.

Districts for entertainment:

Slovenia has thriving nightlife, particularly in cities like Ljubljana, where you can find a wide range of bars, clubs, and entertainment establishments. Although generally safe, it is still advisable to use caution and follow accepted safety procedures:

Drink sensibly: If you use alcohol, do so sparingly and be conscious of your limits. Overindulging in alcohol can cloud your judgment and increase your risk of mishaps or incidents.

b. **Stay with Friends**: It's best to stay with a group of friends if you're out enjoying the nightlife. Make sure everyone gets back to their accommodations safely by keeping an eye out for one another.

Avoid strangers at all costs, particularly if they approach you unexpectedly. Trust your instincts and exercise good judgment. Remove yourself from a situation if it makes you feel uncomfortable or uneasy.

Emergency Contact and Safety Measures:

Emergency Phone Numbers Save the police (113), ambulance (112), and fire department (112) numbers for local emergencies in your phone. In the event of an emergency, call the designated number and give precise details regarding your location and the nature of the situation.

b. **Inform Others**: If you intend to tour Slovenia at night, tell someone you can trust about your itinerary, including the locations you intend to see and the time you anticipate returning. To make sure you're safe, periodically check in with them.

c. **Remain Vigilant:** Be aware of your surroundings and follow your gut feelings. Remove yourself from the situation or ask for help from the appropriate authorities if something doesn't feel right.

Even though Slovenia is generally secure at night, it is important to exercise caution and take the appropriate safety measures. You can have a safe and enjoyable experience exploring Slovenia after dark by adhering to these recommendations, being aware of your surroundings, and using common sense. No matter the time of day or where you are, always prioritize your safety.

Is Slovenia good for International Students?

Slovenia is a great choice for international students looking for a top-notch education and a thriving multicultural environment. Slovenia offers many benefits for students from all over the world, including a friendly atmosphere, reasonable tuition costs, and reputable universities. We will examine Slovenia's appeal to international students in this extensive guide.

Slovenia has a strong educational system that places a strong emphasis on academic excellence and research. Numerous reputable universities and institutions in the nation provide a wide selection of study programs in many different disciplines. Slovenian universities are renowned for their rigorous academic standards, knowledgeable faculty, and cutting-edge infrastructure, giving students access to a top-notch education that is valued around the world.

Studying in Slovenia has many benefits, including its affordable tuition fees when compared to those of many other European nations. Slovenia's affordable tuition rates make it a desirable choice for international students, especially those on a tight budget. The cost of tuition varies according to the course of study and the university, but it is generally less expensive than in other European nations.

Scholarships and Financial Support: Slovenia provides international students with a range of scholarship and financial support options. Deserving students can receive financial aid from the Slovenian government, universities, and other organizations. These scholarships can lessen the financial burden on international students and allow them to concentrate on their studies by helping to cover tuition fees, living expenses, or research projects.

The environment of Diversity: Slovenia welcomes diversity and provides a diverse learning environment for visitors. The nation is home to a burgeoning community of international students, which fosters a vibrant and diverse campus environment. In addition to enhancing the academic experience, interacting with students from various cultures and backgrounds encourages intercultural understanding, tolerance, and lifelong friendships.

English-Taught Programs: To meet the needs of international students, Slovenian universities provide a variety of study programs taught in English. As a result, it is simpler for non-Slovenian speakers to pursue higher education in Slovenia since no language proficiency is necessary. There are numerous academic fields, including the social sciences, natural sciences, engineering, business, and humanities, that offer programs taught in English.

Safe and Friendly Environment: Slovenia is renowned for its peace and safety. Slovenians are renowned for their friendliness and hospitality toward foreign students, and the nation has a low crime rate. You can count on receiving support and a warm welcome during your time studying abroad in Slovenia.

Location in Central Europe: The central European location of Slovenia provides many opportunities for travel and exploration. As a student in Slovenia, you will have quick access to nearby nations like Italy, Austria, Hungary, and Croatia, allowing you to take study breaks to explore new cultures and take in varied landscapes.

Rich Cultural Heritage and Stunning Natural Beauty: Slovenia is known for both its incredible natural beauty and rich cultural heritage. Slovenia offers a variety of attractions for students to explore during their free time, including charming medieval towns, picturesque lakes, breathtaking mountains, and immaculate national parks. Due to the nation's dedication to environmental sustainability and preservation, there are also opportunities for ecotourism and outdoor recreation.

Opportunities for Research and Innovation: Slovenia places a high priority on Research and Innovation. The nation actively promotes student involvement in research initiatives, offering beneficial chances for experiential learning and academic advancement. International students can work with seasoned researchers and advance their respective fields by participating in research activities.

Opportunities for Career Development: Slovenia's expanding economy and strategic location within the European Union offer a favorable environment for career advancement. Slovenia offers valuable work experience, internships, and job placement opportunities for international students who decide to pursue their studies there, both during their studies and after they graduate. Information technology, engineering, tourism, finance, and sustainable development are among the nation's booming industries.

This page was left blank intentionally

8 Beautiful Places You Need to Visit in Slovenia as a First Timer

Slovenia is a nation of astounding natural beauty, charming towns, and rich cultural history. It is a hidden gem in the center of Europe. You will be mesmerized by its various landscapes, gorgeous lakes, endearing castles, and breathtaking mountains as a first-time visitor. This guide will look at eight stunning Slovenian locations that you absolutely must visit.

Lake Bled:

Slovenia's Lake Bled is arguably its most famous and picturesque location. It looks like something out of a fairy tale with its emerald-green lake, an island with a medieval church, and a background of the Julian Alps. Visit the island by boat, wander through the hilltop Bled Castle, or just take in the breathtaking scenery from the lake's shore. A must-try local treat is the renowned Bled cream cake.

Ljubljana:

Ljubljana, the capital of Slovenia, is a charming and energetic city that shouldn't be missed. Its charming old town is pedestrian-friendly and adorned with bright baroque structures, cobblestone streets, and the recognizable Ljubljana Castle that offers sweeping views of the city. Wander along the Ljubljanica River, stop by the Triple Bridge, peruse the nearby markets, and take in the vibrant cafe scene. Visitors are truly mesmerized by Ljubljana's laid-back vibe and stunning architecture.

Triglav National Park:

A visit to Triglav National Park is essential for nature lovers. It is Slovenia's only national park and offers breathtaking views of the Julian Alps. Trek through unpolluted forests, take in cascading waterfalls and be amazed by the lofty peaks. Don't pass up the chance to visit Lake Bohinj, a serene lake surrounded by mountains that is ideal for kayaking, swimming, or just taking in the tranquil atmosphere.

Postojna Cave:

Discover the underground splendors of Postojna Cave, one of Europe's largest cave systems. Take a guided tour to see the stunning Predjama Castle built into the mouth of a cave, as well as the intricate stalactites and stalagmites, underground halls, and more. The journey into the depths of Slovenia's natural wonders is made memorable by the adventure-infused train ride through the cave.

Piran:

The charming town of Piran, which is located on the Adriatic Coast, offers a glimpse of Mediterranean beauty. Its picturesque harbor, Venetian-style architecture, and winding streets all contribute to the town's distinctive coastal atmosphere. Take a stroll along the promenade, stop by Tartini Square, and eat some delicious fresh seafood at a waterfront restaurant. You can also take a boat trip to the breathtaking Slovenian coastline from Piran or explore the nearby Strunjan Nature Reserve.

Škocjan Caves:

Another unprecedented underground marvel, the Škocjan Caverns, a UNESCO World Legacy site, will leave you in wonder. Leave on a directed visit through the huge underground loads, extensions, and cascades. The feature is the Incomparable Corridor, a huge underground gulch that will blow your mind. The Škocjan Caverns feature the uncommon magnificence and force of nature's land developments.

Velika Planina:

Departure to the charming snow-capped knolls of Velika Planina, a high level situated in the Kamnik-Savinja Alps. Arrive at the level by trolley and submerge yourself in the quietness of the pleasant scene. Meander among the customary wooden cottages, partake in the all-encompassing perspectives on the encompassing pinnacles, and experience the nearby shepherd's lifestyle. Velika Planina offers a tranquil retreat and a brief look into Slovenia's rustic appeal.

Maribor:

Situated in the northeastern piece of Slovenia, Maribor is the nation's second-biggest city and a social center point. Investigate the old town's middle-age squares, visit the great Maribor Palace, and meander through the beguiling Loaned region along the Drava Waterway. Try not to miss a visit to the most seasoned plant on the planet, the "Old Plant," and enjoy Maribor's dynamic wine culture. The city likewise has the lively Maribor Theater Celebration, drawing in theater fans from around the world.

These are only a couple of the numerous lovely spots ready to be found in Slovenia. From its captivating lakes and mountains to its enchanting towns and rich social legacy, Slovenia offers a different scope of encounters for first-time guests. Submerge yourself in its normal miracles, investigate its noteworthy destinations, and embrace the glow of Slovenian accommodation. Plan to be astounded by the excellence and appeal that Slovenia brings to the table.

This page was left blank intentionally

When is the Best Time to go Cycling in Slovenia?

Cycling enthusiasts will find paradise in Slovenia, which boasts a variety of landscapes and breathtaking natural beauty. The nation offers a wide variety of cycling opportunities for all skill levels, including strenuous mountain climbs, picturesque coastal routes, and picturesque countryside trails. The ideal time to go cycling in Slovenia, however, depends on several variables, including the weather, the state of the roads, and individual preferences. We will examine the various seasons and how they affect cycling in Slovenia in this in-depth guide.

Spring (March to May):

Cycling in Slovenia is especially enjoyable in the spring when nature is waking up from its winter hibernation. As the temperature rises, the countryside is painted in a rainbow of hues. The weather can be erratic in March and April, with sporadic showers of rain. But as May gets closer, the climate stabilizes and improves. The coastal regions are best explored in the spring, whether by bicycle along the stunning Adriatic coast or by visiting the quaint towns of Piran and Koper.

Summer (June to August):

Slovenia's busiest travel season is summer, which has warm, sunny weather and great cycling conditions. The lengthy daylight hours give plenty of opportunities for long rides and exploration. You can travel into the Julian Alps at this time and attempt some of the difficult mountain passes, like the Vri Pass or the Mangart Pass. The higher altitudes provide relief from the summer heat while still providing breathtaking views of the mountains. Cycling around Lakes Bohinj and Bled during the summer is a great way to take in the picturesque scenery and cool waters.

Autumn (September to November):

Slovenia enjoys a lovely autumn with mild temperatures, clear skies, and breathtaking fall foliage. It's a beautiful time to go cycling because the countryside turns into a kaleidoscopic tapestry. With warm days and chilly evenings, September is especially pleasant. Cycling through Slovenia's wine regions, such as the renowned

Maribor Wine Route or the Vipava Valley, and exploring the vineyards are both ideal activities for this time of year. In comparison to the summer, you can also take advantage of the quieter roads and fewer tourists.

Winter (December to February):

Slovenia experiences a colder winter with snow-covered landscapes, which makes cycling outdoors less feasible. Slovenia offers some fantastic opportunities for experienced cyclists who enjoy fat biking or winter cycling adventures. With specialized trails and paths that are maintained all winter long, the Pohorje Mountains and Kranjska Gora are popular winter cycling destinations. For cyclists who are up for the challenge, these places offer a distinctive and exhilarating experience.

Factors to Consider:

In addition to the seasons, the following points should be taken into account when organizing your cycling trip in Slovenia:

a. **Weather**: Before beginning your cycling adventure, check the weather forecast. Although the weather in Slovenia is generally good for cycling, be ready for sudden changes in the weather, especially in the mountains. Carry the proper equipment and clothing to accommodate varying weather conditions.

b. **Road Conditions:** Pay attention to how well the roads and bike lanes are maintained. Slovenia's main thoroughfares are generally kept up and bicycle-friendly. However, some rural areas might have less bike-friendly infrastructure and narrower roads. Determine your route in advance and pick cycling-friendly roads.

c. **Tourist Season**: When organizing your cycling trip, keep in mind the tourist season. In the summer, especially in July and August, there may be more tourists and traffic on popular cycling routes. For a quieter experience, think about cycling during the off-peak seasons.

d. **Individual Preferences:** When it comes to cycling, everyone has different preferences. While some people might enjoy the challenge of riding through mountainous terrain, others might favor relaxing rides along the coast or through vineyards. When choosing the ideal time to go cycling in Slovenia, keep in mind your level of fitness, cycling expertise, and interests.

This page was left blank intentionally

7 Tricks You Should Never Joke with When Cycling or Biking Trails

Cycling and biking trails offer a fantastic opportunity to experience nature's beauty, learn about the outdoors, and get some exercise. However, it's important to approach these activities cautiously and put safety first. Cycling can be exciting and fun, but there are some maneuvers or actions that should never be done carelessly. This article will go over seven cycling and biking trail jokes you should never make.

Neglecting Protective Gear:

Wearing the proper protective gear is one of the most important aspects of cycling safety. Wearing a helmet is important for preventing head injuries in the event of a fall or accident, so never joke about it or ignore it. Consider wearing gloves, knee and elbow pads, reflective clothing, and other safety equipment in addition to a helmet to improve visibility. Wearing the appropriate equipment, taking safety seriously, and avoiding serious accidents can save lives.

Ignoring Traffic Regulations:

It's important to observe traffic regulations when cycling on shared or public roads. Never make light of disobeying stop signs, traffic lights, or speed limits. Following these guidelines guarantees the security of all road users, including cyclists. Always use a turn signal, stop for pedestrians, and keep a safe distance from moving vehicles. You help create a safer cycling environment for everyone by being a responsible cyclist.

Riding While Intoxicated:

Cycling requires coordination, focus, and quick reflexes. Never make jokes about cycling or do it while intoxicated or using any other impairing substances. Cycling while intoxicated puts your safety and the safety of others in grave danger and significantly increases the risk of accidents. When it comes to cycling, always prioritize sobriety and make sensible choices.

Distracted Riding:

Cycling demands your complete focus and attention. Never make light of or engage in distracted driving, including talking on the phone, playing loud music, or doing other things that divert your attention from the road. You may become unaware of potential dangers or approaching vehicles as a result of these distractions. To ensure a secure and enjoyable cycling experience, remain concentrated and keep your eyes and ears open.

Overestimating Skills:

While it's great to challenge yourself and push your limits, you should never exaggerate your cycling abilities. Choose trails or routes that correspond to your level of experience and be realistic about your abilities. Without the necessary training and experience, attempting difficult or technical trails can result in accidents and injuries. Gradually increase the difficulty while seeking advice from instructors or seasoned cyclists to develop your skills.

Ignoring Bike Maintenance:

For safe cycling, proper bike maintenance is essential. Never make light of not keeping your bike maintained or ignoring potential mechanical problems. Make sure the brakes, tires, chains, and gears on your bike are in good working order regularly. Failure to properly maintain your bike can cause malfunctions while you're riding, endangering your safety. Consult an expert bike shop or seasoned cyclists for advice if you're unsure how to maintain your bike.

Cycling Alone in Remote Areas: Cycling alone in remote or uncharted areas can be dangerous, particularly if you run into problems or have an emergency. Never make light of entering uncharted territory without adequate preparation, navigational equipment, or communication methods. Always let someone know where you're going and when you'll be back if you plan to cycle. To increase safety and support, think about riding with a friend or joining a group.

50 Phrases and basic Slovenian language You Need to Know Before You Visit

It's always beneficial to become familiar with some basic Slovenian phrases before traveling there. Even though English is widely spoken in Slovenia, knowing a few basic phrases can improve your trip and demonstrate respect for the local way of life. In this chapter, I will give you the 50 most important Slovenian words and phrases you'll need to get by on your trip. Let's get going!

1. Greetings, Zdravo (z-DRAH-voh)
2. Dobro jutro (DOH-broh YOO-troh) means good morning.
3. Greetings, Doberdan (DOH-behr DAHN).
4. Greetings and good night, Dober Veer (DOH-behr VEH-cher).
5. Nasvidenje (nahs-VEE-deh-nyeh) means goodbye.
6. Prosim (PROH-seem), please
7. Many thanks - Hvala (HVAH-lah)
8. I'm happy to help. - Nee zah KAI (ni za kaj)

9. Yes, Ja, Ya.

10. "No" - "Ne"

11. Pardon me Oprostite (pronounced oh-PROHS-tee-teh)

12. Oprostite (oh-PROHS-tee-teh): I'm sorry.

13. Are you an English speaker? Govorite angliko? (go VOH-ree-teh anh-GLESH-koh?)

14. I don't comprehend "Ne razumem" (neh rah-ZOO-mem)

15. Could you please assist me? Prosim mi lahko pomagate? (proh-seem mee LAH-koh poh-MAH-gah-teh?)

16. Where is that? - Kje je...? (Okay, yeah?)

17. What is the price? Koliko stane? koh-LEE-koh STAH-neh

18. I desire to... "Rad/a bi imel/a" The phrase "rahd/ah bee ee-MEL/ah"

19. Can you suggest a reputable eatery? - Mi lahko priporoite good dining experience? (mee LAH-ko pree poh-ROH-chee-teh DOH-broh rehs-tah-VRAH-tsee-yoh?)

20. What hotel locations are there? How far away is the hotel? (Kay Lah Koh New Year's Eve Ho Tehl?)

21. I need a doctor, so please help Poh-TREH-boo-yem, z-DRAHV-nee-kah

22. The restroom is where? How is the situation? Kay Yeh Strah Neesh Cheh?

23. Cheers! No problem! (no ZDRAH-vee!)

24. Tell me your name. How do you feel? KAH-ko vahm yeh EE-meh?

25. My name is (MOH-yeh EE-meh yeh) Moje ime je.

26. What's up? - How are you? (KAH-koh st?)

27. I'm good, thanks. Do well, thank you. (DOH-broh sehm, HVAH-lah) Could you please assist me? "Mi lahko pomagate?" Mee Lah Koh Poh Mah Gah Teh

28. How do I purchase tickets? "Kje lahko kupim vstopnice?" you ask. Kay Lah Koo Peem VSTOH Pee?

29. I cherish Slovenia Oboujem Slovenijo (oh-BOH-zhoo-yem SLOH-veh-nee-yo)

30. Could I take a picture? - Laho photographam? (LAH-koh FOO-toh GRAH FEE-rahm?)

31. When is it now? How much is too much? Koh-LEE-koh Yeh OO-rah

32. Where do I locate a taxi? "Kje lahko najdem taksi," Kay Lah Koh New Year's Eve?

33. I'm disoriented - Izgubil/a sem Is there Wi-Fi in this area? Do you have Wi-Fi, Ali? (AH-lee, Wi-Fi too?)

34. Can you suggest a dish from the area? "Mi lahko priporoite lokalno jed," you ask? (mee Lah Koh Pree Poh Roh Chee Teh Lo Kal No Yeht?)

35. Asthma affects me... - There are no allergies here. /sehm ah-LEHR-gee-chehn/

36. Is this seat occupied? - Je ta zaseden sede? Yeh tah seh dehn zah seh dehn?

37. Where is the nearest pharmacy? When will the lekarno arrive? (kay Lah Koh New Year's Eve leh Kahr Noh?)

38. Can you suggest any local points of interest? Mi Lahko Prporoite Kakne Local Znamenitosti? (mee LAH-koh pree-poh-ROH-chee-tee Teh KAHK-shneh loh-KAHL-neh znah-meh-nee-TOHS-tee?)

39. Exists a bank in the area? "Are you a bank in Bliin?" (AH-lee yeh too blee-ZEE-nee?

40. Where can I find...? (KAH-koh PREE-dehm do...) Kako pridem do

41. Can I use a credit card to pay? - How do I use my credit card? (LAH-ko PLAH-chahm s kreh-DEET-noh KAR-tee-tso?)

42. How is the weather right now? - How long has the day been? (KAHK-shno you VREH-me DAH-nehs?)

43. Please speak more slowly. Govorite poasneje, please say? (proh-seem go-VOH-ree-teh poh-CHAH-sneh-yeh?)

44. Ne jem mesa, I don't eat meat Neh yehm Mesa

45. Could you suggest a good hiking route? - Mi lahko priporoite good pohodnikov pot? Mee LAH-koh pree-poh-ROH-chee-teh DOH-broh poh-HOHD-neesh-koh poht

46. Is there a gas station nearby? Alias, are you the Bencinska rpalka? (AH-lee yeh too behn-tseen-skah CHUR-pahl-kah?)

47. Could you give me directions? How may I help you with your navodili? (mee Lah Koh Poh Mah Teh Z Nah Voh Dee Lee?)

48. Enjoy your day! Leap forward, please! (Let me help you, please!)

By mastering these words, you'll not only have a more enjoyable trip to Slovenia but you'll also be demonstrating respect for the local language and culture. Slovenians value efforts made to learn even a few fundamental phrases. So go ahead and practice these words and phrases before you travel to Slovenia and take advantage of the chance to communicate with people there and fully experience the country.

This page was left blank intentionally

7 Easy Ways to Save Money for Your Trip

Spending less money is frequently a top priority when organizing a trip. There are several simple ways to save money for your trip, whether you're traveling on a budget or simply want to make the most of your money. You can ensure that you have more financial flexibility and can take pleasure in your travel experience without going over budget by putting these strategies into practice. We'll go over seven simple ways to cut costs on your trip in this guide. Let's start now!

Establish a budget: Setting up a budget is the first step in saving money for your trip. Estimate the total cost of your trip, taking into account lodging, travel, meals, activities, and any other costs. Next, figure out how much you must put aside each month until your trip to achieve your goal. You can keep track of your spending and find areas where you can make cuts to save more money by creating a clear budget.

Cut back on unnecessary spending by carefully examining your monthly budget to find areas where you can make savings. Take into account lowering or removing expenses like eating out, entertainment subscriptions, or unnecessary shopping. Put the money you would have spent on these expenses in your travel fund instead. When you're having fun on your trip, it might require some sacrifices, but it will be worthwhile.

Automate your saving process to make saving money a top priority. Create a separate savings account for your travel fund and set up an automatic transfer from your checking account to it. This will enable you to save money without even having to think about it. It's an easy and efficient way to gradually increase your travel budget.

Reduce transportation costs: One of the biggest out-of-pocket expenses on a trip is frequent transportation. By being flexible with your travel dates, try to find ways to reduce your transportation costs. Booking your flights on a weekday or outside of the busiest travel times can frequently result in lower costs. Additionally, to find the best offers on train or flight tickets, think about using price comparison websites or subscribing to fare alerts.

Options for lodging: Another place where you can cut costs is lodging. Consider alternatives like hostels, guesthouses, or vacation rentals instead of spending a lot of money on hotels. These choices can offer a distinctive and genuine travel experience and are frequently more affordable. Additionally, think about making your hotel reservations in advance to benefit from early bird discounts or other special offers.

Prepare your food instead of eating out, which can quickly drain your travel budget. Instead of eating out every meal, think about cooking some of your meals to save money on food costs. Take advantage of the kitchens if your accommodations have them and make your breakfast and lunch. By shopping at nearby markets and attempting to prepare traditional dishes, you can not only save money but also have fun getting to know the local cuisine.

Before your trip, do some research on the activities and sights you want to see and then order them according to your budget. It's important to pick attractions that fit your interests and financial constraints because some may charge expensive entrance fees. Additionally, look for free or inexpensive activities like visiting your neighborhood markets, parks, or cultural events. These can offer priceless experiences without draining your wallet.

10-Day Slovenia Itinerary Guide

You can experience Slovenia's varied landscapes, rich history, charming towns, and vibrant culture by organizing a 10-day trip there. Every traveler can find something to enjoy in Slovenia, from taking in the breathtaking natural beauty of Lake Bled and Triglav National Park to discovering the charming capital city of Ljubljana. We'll walk you through the must-see locations in this 10-day itinerary guide and point out the top attractions in each city. Let's start now!

Day 1:

Ljubljana Start your journey in Ljubljana, Slovenia's capital. Spend the day discovering the quaint old town, which is distinguished by its vibrant Baroque structures, cobblestone streets, and vibrant café scene. Visit Ljubljana Castle for sweeping city views, stroll along the lovely

Ljubljanica River, and don't skip the vivacious Central Market for a taste of the regional cuisine.

Day 2:

Lake Bled - Visit one of Slovenia's most well-known tourist destinations, Lake Bled. Enjoy the magnificent lake's emerald-green waters and the picturesque island with its church on top. Obtain a breathtaking view by ascending to the church on the island after a traditional Pletna boat ride. A must-try local treat is the renowned Bled cream cake.

Day 3:

Triglav National Park - Set out on a day trip to the Julian Alps' Triglav National Park. Discover the pristine alpine lands, go on a hike to the magnificent Savica Waterfall, and be in awe of the stunning Lake Bohinj, which is encircled by mountains. Also available to those who enjoy the outdoors are rafting, canyoning, and paragliding.

Day 4:

Predjama Castle and Postojna Cave - One of the largest karst cave systems in the world is the fascinating Postojna Cave. Take a guided tour of the underground wonderland to see the stunning stalactite formations. Then, proceed to Predjama Castle, a magnificent fortress that was carved out of a cave's opening and offers a singular architectural wonder.

Day 5:

Piran - Visit the Adriatic Sea coastal settlement of Piran. Explore the city's winding medieval streets, gaze upon the magnificent Tartini Square, and take in the breathtaking views from the city walls. Enjoy the beach, a meal of succulent seafood, and the enchanting Mediterranean ambience of this coastal treasure.

Day 6:

Lipica Stud Farm and Kocjan Caves - Discover the enormous stalactites and underground canyons of the Kocjan Caves, a UNESCO World Heritage site. Take a guided tour to experience this natural wonder's breathtaking beauty. After that, see a classy horse show at the Lipica Stud Farm, the home of the Lipizzaner horses.

Day 7:

Ptuj and Maribor Maribor, Slovenia's second-largest city, is to the east. Take a stroll along the riverfront, visit the magnificent Maribor Cathedral, and explore the city's historic center. Continue to Ptuj, one of Slovenia's oldest towns. Explore the medieval castle that has been preserved, stroll through the quaint old town, and sample some local wines at the Ptuj Wine Cellar.

Day 8:

Velika Planina and Logar Valley - Visit the Logar Valley, a picturesque alpine valley renowned for its unspoiled landscapes, waterfalls, and hiking trails, to fully appreciate Slovenia's breathtaking natural beauty. Enjoy the peace of the area by going on a leisurely hike. Go to Velika Planina next, a remarkable mountain plateau dotted with old-fashioned shepherd huts. Discover the traditional way of life while taking in the expansive mountain views.

Day 9:

Lake Bohinj - Visit Lake Bohinj, a tranquil and less crowded alternative to Lake Bled, as you head back to the Julian Alps. Walk around the lake at your own pace, rent a boat to explore its clear waters, or hike to nearby lookout points for breathtaking views. Take advantage of the chance to travel on the Vogel Cable Car for sweeping views of the Julian Alps.

Day 10:

Radovljica and Vintgar Gorge - Visit Vintgar Gorge, a breathtaking natural wonder close to Bled, to round out your journey. Take a stroll along the wooden paths and bridges while taking in the turquoise waters and cascading waterfalls. After that, explore the quaint town of Radovljica, which is renowned for its exquisite gingerbread and well-preserved medieval old town.

However, you are free to change the schedule by your preferences and available time. Slovenia is an excellent country to explore and make lifelong memories because of its small size, which makes getting from one place to another simple.

This page was left blank intentionally

What Does Slovenia Looks Like Every Months with Activities: A Month-to-Month Guide

Every month has its distinct charm and opportunities for discovery. In this thorough guide, we'll walk you through Slovenia's four distinct seasons and highlight the things to do and see in each one.

Slovenia in January:

The snow-covered landscapes of Slovenia in January make for a winter wonderland. With skiers and snowboarders taking advantage of the immaculate slopes, the Julian Alps and the ski resorts of Kranjska Gora, Vogel, and Krvavec come alive. In the lovely valleys and forests, cross-country skiing and snowshoeing are popular winter sports. Ljubljana offers a variety of winter festivals that include ice skating, traditional markets, and fun activities for those looking for cultural experiences.

Slovenia in February:

Slovenia's wintery atmosphere continues in February, with great skiing conditions and lots of opportunities for winter sports. Pohorje and Maribor's ski slopes draw tourists with their well-maintained ski runs and inviting mountain huts. In the Julian Alps, ice climbers can test their skills on frozen waterfalls. Relaxation and warmth are provided by indoor pursuits like touring Ljubljana's museums and art galleries or luxuriating in thermal spas like Terme ate.

Slovenia in March:

As winter gives way to spring, Slovenia in March offers a mix of winter and the first indications of the natural world waking up. While lower regions like the Karst and Istria experience milder temperatures, higher-altitude resorts still offer skiing. The magical underground world of Postojna Cave and Kocjan Caves is best explored in March. Trekkers can enter Triglav National Park to take in the snow-capped peaks and breathtaking alpine scenery.

April heralds the start of spring in Slovenia, bringing with it warmer weather and blooming landscapes. It's a great time to visit the nation's picturesque countryside. Wine lovers can partake in wine tastings and cellar tours as the vineyards of the Primorska and Posavje regions come alive with vibrant colors. Nature lovers can explore the magnificent Lake Bohinj, go on a hike through the lovely Logar Valley, or go cycling through the picturesque countryside.

Slovenia in May:

The spring blooms are in full bloom in May, making it a lovely time to visit Slovenia. The vibrant flowers and outdoor cafes that line the riverbanks of Ljubljana's capital city serve as a visual representation of its beauty. It's a great month for outdoor pursuits like kayaking on the clear rivers, cycling through the Ljubljana Marshes, and hiking in the Soa Valley. The picturesque horse shows at Lipica Stud Farm are captivating, and the Mediterranean charm of Piran and Portoro's coastal towns beckons.

Slovenia in June:

June is a great month to explore Slovenia's natural wonders because of the longer days and pleasant weather. The trails in the Julian Alps lead to magnificent peaks and alpine meadows, providing wonderful hiking opportunities. Adventure seekers are invited to go rafting and canyoning on the emerald-green Soa River. Both the Predjama Castle and the Postojna Cave are well-known tourist destinations. Festivals and beach activities animate the coastal region, and Lake Bled sparkles in the summer sun.

Slovenia in July:

With warm temperatures and a lively atmosphere, July marks the height of Slovenia's summer season. The Slovenian coast becomes a popular destination for sunbathers, with beach resorts providing a variety of water sports. For lovers of swimming and boating, Lake Bled turns into a paradise. The Karst region welcomes visitors to explore its underground caves and take advantage of the chilly temperatures inside, while the Julian Alps provide breathtaking hikes and climbing opportunities.

August in Slovenia:

August in Slovenia maintains a summery atmosphere, drawing tourists with its pleasant weather and exciting events. Several cultural festivals, including music concerts and traditional performances, are held in the seaside towns of Piran and Portoro. Performances of music, theater, and dance are on display in the capital city during the Ljubljana Summer Festival. Outdoor enthusiasts can hike to Triglav, Slovenia's highest peak, or go cycling through the picturesque countryside.

Slovenia in September:

As the summer crowds thin out and the landscapes turn golden, September is a great month to travel to Slovenia. Grape harvesting is in full swing in the vineyards, and wine regions like the Vipava Valley and Gorika Brda host wine-tasting events. Hikers can take pleasure in the trails in the tranquil surroundings of the Triglav National Park as it displays its autumnal hues. A leisurely boat ride on the picture-perfect Lake Bled or a stroll along its serene shores are ideal.

Slovenia in October:

October brings Slovenia's stunning autumn foliage, which turns the surroundings into a picturesque work of art.

Hiking in the lush red, orange, and yellow forests of the Julian Alps and Pohorje Mountains provides enjoyable outdoor experiences. Visitors can enjoy the flavors of freshly pressed grape juice while the wine regions are still busy with harvest activities. Ljubljana, the country's capital, embraces the fall season with cozier cafes and cultural activities.

Winter in Slovenia begins in November, bringing with it colder temperatures and the potential for snow in higher elevations. It is the perfect time to explore the charming towns and cities with their preserved historical architecture, such as Maribor, Ptuj, and kofja Loka. Thermal resorts such as Terme Olimia and Terme Ptuj provide a cozy retreat, and the Christmas markets in Ljubljana and other towns start to set up, fostering a festive atmosphere.

Slovenia in December:

With the holiday spirit in full swing, December is a magical time to visit Slovenia. A charming atmosphere is created by the holiday accents and Christmas markets in Ljubljana. Families can enjoy sledding and snowball fights in the snowy landscapes, and the ski resorts are bustling with winter sports enthusiasts. A glimpse into Slovenian holiday customs can be found at the traditional holiday markets in Ptuj and Radovljica, as well as in the Alpine towns of Bled and Kranjska Gora.

Slovenia offers a variety of experiences and activities all year long, with each month bringing its special beauty and charm. Everyone can find something to enjoy in Slovenia's diverse landscapes and dynamic cities, whether they are outdoor enthusiasts, cultural explorers, or nature lovers. So make sure to plan your trip appropriately and get ready to be mesmerized by Slovenia's breathtaking natural beauty, rich cultural history, and gracious people.

This page was left blank intentionally

Packing Essentials for Slovenia

It's important to pack thoughtfully for your trip to Slovenia to make sure you have everything you need for a relaxing and enjoyable stay. A flexible and well-planned packing list is required due to the country's diverse landscapes, fluctuating weather patterns, and variety of activities. We will list the necessary items you should think about including on your packing list for Slovenia in this guide.

Clothing:

Layered clothing: Because Slovenian weather can be erratic, it's a good idea to pack a variety of clothing that can be worn under other items. This includes long-sleeved tops, sweaters or fleece, and a waterproof jacket in addition to lightweight, breathable shirts.

- Comfortable walking shoes are a necessity in Slovenia because of the country's stunning scenery and abundance of outdoor activities. Make sure they are cozy and offer adequate traction for various surfaces.

- Pack swimwear if you intend to visit coastal areas or take advantage of thermal spas and lakes.
- Hat and sunglasses: During the summer, shield your eyes from the sun's rays by bringing a hat and sunglasses.
- Gloves and scarf: It's a good idea to pack gloves and a warm scarf during the colder months, especially in the alpine regions, to stay warm in the chilly temperatures.
- Having a few outfits that work in both casual and more formal settings is a good idea because Slovenia has a mix of both.
- Outdoor gear: daypack or backpack: For day trips and other outdoor activities, a convenient daypack is required. Pick one with a supportive back and lots of storage.
- Water bottle: Bring a reusable water bottle with you on your adventures to stay hydrated.
- Sunscreen: Use it to shield your skin from the sun's rays when outdoors, especially in the summer.
- Use insect repellent if you intend to explore the countryside or forests to avoid getting bitten by mosquitoes or ticks.

- Binoculars: Slovenia is a fantastic location for birdwatching and nature observation due to its diverse wildlife and beautiful landscapes. Packing a pair of binoculars could improve your trip.

Travel essentials and documents:

Make sure you have a passport that is at least six months old and a valid visa. According to your nationality, find out if you need a visa to enter Slovenia and make sure you have the required paperwork.

- Travel insurance: It is strongly advised to have travel insurance that includes coverage for lost luggage, trip cancellations, and medical emergencies.
- Copies of significant paperwork: Your passport, visa, travel insurance, and other important documents should be copied or photographed. To prevent loss or theft, store them apart from the originals.
- Money and cards: For convenience, carry a combination of cash and cards, such as a credit or debit card. To prevent any problems with card usage, make sure to let your bank know about your travel plans.

- Travel adapters: If your devices have different plug types, you should pack a universal travel adapter because Slovenia uses the Europlug (Type C and F) electrical outlets.

Accessories and electronics:

- Camera and extras: Slovenia's breathtaking scenery and architectural marvels make for fantastic photo opportunities. Your camera, along with any extra lenses, batteries, memory cards, and chargers, should be brought.
- Pack a portable power bank to keep your electronic devices charged while you're on the go.
- Mobile phone and charger: Ensure that your phone is Slovenian network compatible and unlocked. Bring a charger, and think about getting a local SIM card for calls and data.
- If you depend on the internet a lot, think about packing a portable Wi-Fi hotspot so you can stay connected while traveling.

Medicines and personal care products:

- Toiletries: Bring your preferred personal care products, such as toothpaste, a toothbrush, shampoo, conditioner, and any other items you might need.

- Medication: If you need to take prescription medication, make sure you have enough for the entire trip. Carrying a small first aid kit with basic supplies like bandages, painkillers, and any required prescription medications is also a good idea.

Additional Items:

- travel manual or atlas: Even though there are many useful digital resources, a physical travel guidebook or map can help navigate and learn about Slovenia's attractions.
- Passport locks To protect your belongings while traveling, lock your luggage with travel locks.
- A travel pillow and eye mask can make your trip more comfortable if you have a long flight or expect to need rest while you're traveling.
- Snacks: Bring some quick snacks for the trip or for while you're out exploring Slovenia's natural beauty.
- Keep in mind to pack lightly and take the airline weight restrictions into account. Check the weather forecast for the days of your trip and make

necessary adjustments to your packing list. It's always a good idea to pack items that will make your trip comfortable and enjoyable as well as items that will be prepared for various scenarios.

10 Best Place to Stay in Slovenia for Affordable Price

When planning a trip to Slovenia, finding affordable accommodation is often a top priority. Luckily, Slovenia offers a range of options that cater to different budgets without compromising on comfort and quality. Whether you're looking for a cozy guesthouse in the countryside or a budget-friendly hotel in the city, there are plenty of affordable places to stay in Slovenia. In this guide, we will explore ten of the best places to stay in Slovenia that offer affordable prices without sacrificing amenities or location.

Ljubljana - Hostel Celica:

Features: Hostel Celica is a unique accommodation option located in the heart of Ljubljana. It was once a prison and has been converted into a vibrant hostel with individual prison cells turned into comfortable rooms. The hostel features a communal kitchen, bar, and courtyard.

Pros: Affordable rates, central location, unique and quirky atmosphere, social and communal spaces, friendly staff.

Cons: Shared facilities, and limited privacy in dormitory-style rooms.

Price: Prices start at around €20 per night for a bed in a dormitory room.

Bled - Garden House Bled:

Features: Garden House Bled is a charming guesthouse located near Lake Bled. It offers cozy rooms with private bathrooms and a shared kitchen. The guesthouse has a beautiful garden with outdoor seating and a barbecue area.

Pros: Affordable rates, peaceful location, close to Lake Bled, friendly and helpful hosts, access to a shared kitchen, charming garden.

Cons: Limited on-site amenities, limited availability during peak season.

Price: Prices start at around €40 per night for a double room.

Piran - Guest House PachaMama Pleasant Stay:

Features: Guest House PachaMama is a delightful guesthouse situated in the picturesque town of Piran on the Slovenian coast. It offers comfortable rooms with private bathrooms and a shared kitchen. The guesthouse has a terrace with panoramic views of the town.

Pros: Affordable rates, great location in Piran's old town, friendly and welcoming hosts, access to a shared kitchen, and stunning views from the terrace.

Cons: Limited availability, limited on-site facilities.

Price: Prices start at around €50 per night for a double room.

Maribor - Guesthouse Mlada Lipa:

Features: Guesthouse Mlada Lipa is a family-run guesthouse located in the wine region of Maribor. It offers cozy rooms with private bathrooms and an on-site restaurant serving traditional Slovenian cuisine. The guesthouse has a garden and terrace.

Pros: Affordable rates, tranquil location, friendly and attentive staff, on-site restaurant, beautiful garden, free parking.

Cons: Limited availability, remote location for those wanting to explore Maribor city center.

Price: Prices start at around €60 per night for a double room.

Lake Bohinj - Hostel pod Voglom:

Features: Hostel Pod Voglom is a budget-friendly accommodation option situated near Lake Bohinj. It offers dormitory-style rooms with shared bathrooms. The hostel has a restaurant, bar, and a terrace with stunning lake views.

Pros: Affordable rates, beautiful lakefront location, on-site restaurant and bar, social and communal spaces, breathtaking views.

Cons: Shared facilities, and limited privacy in dormitory rooms.

Price: Prices start at around €25 per night for a bed in a dormitory room.

Ptuj - Hotel Poetovio:

Features: Hotel Poetovio is a comfortable and affordable hotel located in the historic town of Ptuj. It offers spacious rooms with private bathrooms, an on-site restaurant, and a wellness center with a sauna and hot tub.

Pros: Affordable rates, convenient location in Ptuj, comfortable rooms, on-site restaurant and wellness facilities, free parking.

Cons: Limited availability, and fewer on-site amenities compared to larger hotels.

Price: Prices start at around €70 per night for a double room.

Kranjska Gora - Hotel Kotnik:

Features: Hotel Kotnik is a family-run hotel situated in the popular mountain resort town of Kranjska Gora. It offers comfortable rooms with private bathrooms, an on-site restaurant serving Slovenian cuisine, and a wellness center with a sauna and indoor pool.

Pros: Affordable rates, great location in Kranjska Gora, friendly and helpful staff, on-site restaurant and wellness facilities.

Cons: Limited availability, popular tourist destination.

Price: Prices start at around €80 per night for a double room.

Radovljica - Gostilna Lectar:

Features: Gostilna Lectar is a traditional guesthouse located in the charming town of Radovljica. It offers cozy rooms with private bathrooms and an on-site restaurant serving Slovenian specialties. The guesthouse is known for its gingerbread-making tradition.

Pros: Affordable rates, historic and picturesque location, traditional atmosphere, on-site restaurant, unique gingerbread-making experience.

Cons: Limited availability, limited on-site facilities.

Price: Prices start at around €70 per night for a double room.

Bohinjska Bistrica - Hostel Mama Minka:

Features: Hostel Mama Minka is a budget-friendly hostel located in Bohinjska Bistrica, close to Lake Bohinj. It offers dormitory-style rooms with shared bathrooms and a communal kitchen. The hostel has a cozy common area and an outdoor terrace.

Pros: Affordable rates, close to Lake Bohinj, communal kitchen, social and communal spaces, friendly and helpful staff.

Cons: Shared facilities, and limited privacy in dormitory rooms.

Price: Prices start at around €20 per night for a bed in a dormitory room.

Portorož - Hostel Portorož:

Features: Hostel Portorož is a budget-friendly accommodation option located in the coastal town of Portorož. It offers dormitory-style rooms with shared bathrooms and a common kitchen. The hostel has a terrace with sea views.

Pros: Affordable rates, close to the beach, communal kitchen, social and communal spaces, and sea views.

Cons: Shared facilities, and limited privacy in dormitory rooms.

Price: Prices start at around €25 per night for a bed in a dormitory room.

This page was left blank intentionally

10 Best Luxuries Hotel to Stay in Slovenia

When it comes to indulgent and luxurious accommodations, Slovenia offers a range of options that provide top-notch amenities, stunning views, and impeccable service. Whether you're seeking a lavish hotel in the heart of the city or a secluded retreat in the countryside, Slovenia has something to cater to every taste. In this guide, we will explore ten of the best luxury hotels to stay in Slovenia, highlighting their features, pros, cons, and approximate prices per night.

Kempinski Palace Portorož:

Features: Kempinski Palace Portorož is a five-star luxury hotel located on the Adriatic coast. It features elegant rooms and suites with sea views, a private beach, a spa and wellness center, multiple restaurants, and a casino.

Pros: Stunning seafront location, luxurious rooms and suites, extensive spa and wellness facilities, fine dining options, attentive service.

Cons: Higher price range, popular tourist destination.

Price: Prices start at around €250 per night.

InterContinental Ljubljana:

Features: InterContinental Ljubljana is a modern and stylish luxury hotel situated in the heart of Ljubljana. It offers spacious rooms and suites, a rooftop restaurant and bars with panoramic city views, a wellness center, and meeting facilities.

Pros: Prime location in the city center, contemporary and well-appointed rooms, rooftop dining with breathtaking views, and excellent amenities.

Cons: Higher price range, limited availability during peak season.

Price: Prices start at around €200 per night.

Grand Hotel Union Ljubljana:

Features: Grand Hotel Union Ljubljana is a historic five-star hotel located near the main square in Ljubljana. It offers elegant rooms and suites, a wellness center with a pool, multiple dining options, and conference facilities.

Pros: Central location, classic and luxurious ambiance, excellent wellness facilities, fine dining options.

Cons: Higher price range, limited availability during peak season.

Price: Prices start at around €150 per night.

Chateau Eza:

Features: Chateau Eza is a boutique luxury hotel nestled in the village of Izola. It offers charming rooms and suites with sea views, a gourmet restaurant, a terrace, and a wine cellar.

Pros: Idyllic coastal location, intimate and romantic ambiance, exquisite dining experience, personalized service.

Cons: Limited number of rooms, remote location for those seeking city amenities.

Price: Prices start at around €300 per night.

Hotel Grad Otočec:

Features: Hotel Grad Otočec is a castle hotel situated on a small island in the middle of the Krka River. It offers luxurious rooms and suites, a gourmet restaurant, a wellness center, and a golf course.

Pros: Unique castle setting, tranquil and picturesque surroundings, exceptional dining options, extensive wellness facilities.

Cons: Remote location, limited availability.

Price: Prices start at around €200 per night.

Hotel Cubo:

Features: Hotel Cubo is a boutique luxury hotel located in the center of Ljubljana. It offers stylish and contemporary rooms, a gourmet restaurant, a bar, and a fitness center.

Pros: Central location, modern and chic design, excellent dining options, personalized service.

Cons: Limited on-site amenities, limited availability.

Price: Prices start at around €180 per night.

Vila Bled:

Features: Vila Bled is a historic villa-turned-luxury hotel situated on the shores of Lake Bled. It offers elegant rooms and suites, a lakefront terrace, a private beach, and a fine dining restaurant.

Pros: Stunning lakefront location, intimate and serene atmosphere, beautiful views, gourmet dining experience.

Cons: Limited number of rooms, limited availability during peak season.

Price: Prices start at around €250 per night.

Hotel Triglav Bled:

Features: Hotel Triglav Bled is a boutique hotel located in the charming town of Bled. It offers comfortable and stylish rooms, a restaurant with panoramic lake views, a wellness center, and easy access to outdoor activities.

Pros: Beautiful lakefront location, cozy and inviting ambiance, breathtaking views, wellness facilities.

Cons: Limited on-site amenities, limited availability during peak season.

Price: Prices start at around €150 per night.

Hotel Kempinski Palace, Portorož:

Features: Hotel Kempinski Palace is a luxury hotel located on the Slovenian coast in Portorož. It offers spacious and elegant rooms and suites, a private beach, a spa and wellness center, several restaurants, and a casino.

Pros: Prime seafront location, luxurious accommodations, extensive spa facilities, and multiple dining options.

Cons: Higher price range, popular tourist destination.

Price: Prices start at around €250 per night.

Hotel Livada Prestige:

Features: Hotel Livada Prestige is a luxury hotel located in the spa town of Moravske Toplice. It offers comfortable and well-appointed rooms, a wellness center, an outdoor thermal pool, and access to the spa's medical and wellness services.

Pros: Relaxing thermal spa environment, modern and comfortable rooms, extensive wellness facilities, and thermal pools.

Cons: Limited availability, remote location for those seeking city amenities.

Price: Prices start at around €200 per night.

15 Top Delicious Food You Should Try in Slovenia

Whether you're exploring the local specialties or indulging in regional delicacies, Slovenian cuisine will surely leave you satisfied. Remember to savor the flavors, embrace the culinary traditions, and enjoy the culinary journey through Slovenia. Here are the ten (10) most delicious food you should try in Slovenia;

Potica:

Potica is a traditional Slovenian rolled pastry made of sweet yeast dough filled with various fillings, such as walnuts, poppy seeds, cottage cheese, or chocolate.

Pros: Rich and indulgent flavors, unique pastry-making technique, popular traditional dessert.

Cons: Can be quite sweet and heavy for some, and may not suit dietary restrictions.

Cost: Prices vary depending on the size and filling, ranging from €10 to €20 per potica.

Štruklji:

Štruklji is rolled dumplings made from thin dough and filled with various ingredients, such as cottage cheese, spinach, bacon, or nuts. They are usually served with melted butter or sour cream.

Pros: Versatile dish with various filling options, comforting and satisfying, a traditional Slovenian specialty.

Cons: Can be quite filling, may not suit dietary restrictions.

Cost: Prices vary depending on the filling and the restaurant, ranging from €8 to €15 per plate.

Kranjska Klobasa:

Kranjska Klobasa, also known as Carniolan sausage, is a Slovenian traditional sausage made from high-quality pork and flavored with garlic and pepper. It is typically served with sauerkraut and mustard.

Pros: Juicy and flavorful sausage, a symbol of Slovenian culinary heritage, popular street food option.

Cons: High in calories and fat, may not suit vegetarian or vegan diets.

Cost: Prices vary depending on the location and serving size, ranging from €5 to €10 per portion.

Prekmurska Gibanica:

Prekmurska Gibanica is a layered pastry dessert originating from the Prekmurje region of Slovenia. It consists of poppy seeds, walnuts, apples, and cottage cheese, all layered between filo pastry.

Pros: Unique combination of flavors, sweet and indulgent, a beloved traditional dessert.

Cons: Can be quite heavy and sweet for some, and may not suit dietary restrictions.

Cost: Prices vary depending on the size and bakery, ranging from €10 to €20 per gibanica.

Idrijski Žlikrofi:

Idrijski Žlikrofi is a traditional Slovenian dumpling filled with potatoes, onion, and herbs. They are shaped like small hats and often served with melted butter or a light sauce.

Pros: Distinctive and flavorful dumplings, a specialty of the Idrija region, visually appealing presentation.

Cons: Can be time-consuming to make, and limited availability outside Slovenia.

Cost: Prices vary depending on the restaurant, ranging from €8 to €15 per plate.

Belokranjska Pogača:

Belokranjska Pogača is a round flatbread topped with a mixture of lard, cracklings, and garlic. It is then baked until crispy and golden.

Pros: Crispy and flavorful bread, a regional specialty of the Bela Krajina region, versatile as a snack or accompaniment.

Cons: High in fat and calories, may not suit dietary restrictions.

Cost: Prices vary depending on the size and bakery, ranging from €5 to €10 per pogača.

Ajdovi Žganci:

Ajdovi Žganci are buckwheat spoonbread dumplings, typically served with cracklings, sauerkraut, or other savory toppings. They have a distinct nutty flavor and a slightly grainy texture.

Pros: Nutritious and gluten-free option, unique flavor profile, a traditional Slovenian dish.

Cons: May not appeal to those who are not fond of buckwheat flavor, limited availability outside Slovenia.

Cost: Prices vary depending on the restaurant, ranging from €8 to €15 per plate.

Skuta:

Skuta is a type of Slovenian cottage cheese, often enjoyed as a spread on bread or used as an ingredient in various dishes, such as pastries or desserts.

Pros: Creamy and tangy cheese, versatile in cooking and baking, popular in traditional Slovenian recipes.

Cons: May not suit lactose-intolerant individuals or those with dairy allergies.

Cost: Prices vary depending on the brand and quantity, ranging from €2 to €5 per package.

Soča Trout:

Soča Trout is a freshwater fish native to the Soča River in Slovenia. It is known for its delicate texture and mild flavor, often prepared grilled or pan-fried.

Pros: Fresh and flavorful fish, a specialty of the Soča Valley, rich in omega-3 fatty acids.

Cons: Availability may be limited outside the region, and higher prices compared to other fish varieties.

Cost: Prices vary depending on the restaurant and size of the portion, ranging from €15 to €30 per plate.

Šmorn:

Šmorn, also known as Kaiserschmarrn, is a fluffy pancake dessert served in torn pieces and sprinkled with powdered sugar. It is often accompanied by fruit compote or jam.

Pros: Light and fluffy pancake texture, sweet and satisfying, popular dessert option.

Cons: Can be quite sweet and high in calories, may not suit dietary restrictions.

Cost: Prices vary depending on the restaurant, ranging from €8 to €15 per plate.

Kraški Pršut:

Kraški Pršut is a Slovenian dry-cured ham made from carefully selected pork and aged in the Karst region. It is thinly sliced and served as an appetizer or in sandwiches.

Pros: Rich and savory flavor, high-quality cured meat, a regional delicacy.

Cons: Limited availability outside Slovenia, may not suit vegetarian or vegan diets.

Cost: Prices vary depending on the brand and quantity, ranging from €15 to €30 per 100 grams.

Bleki:

Bleki is a traditional Slovenian dish consisting of rolled slices of pork belly, filled with a mixture of minced meat, onions, and spices. It is then slow-cooked until tender and served with various sides.

Pros: Tender and flavorful pork dish, a hearty traditional Slovenian specialty.

Cons: High in calories and fat, may not suit vegetarian or vegan diets.

Cost: Prices vary depending on the restaurant, ranging from €12 to €25 per plate.

Fritule:

Fritule is small deep-fried dough balls, often flavored with citrus zest, rum, and raisins. They are typically dusted with powdered sugar and served as a sweet treat.

Pros: Light and fluffy dough, sweet and aromatic flavors, popular during festive seasons.

Cons: Fried and high in calories, may not suit dietary restrictions.

Cost: Prices vary depending on the bakery or street vendor, ranging from €2 to €5 per portion.

Žganci with Sour Milk:

Žganci with Sour Milk is a traditional Slovenian dish made of buckwheat spoonbread dumplings, served with sour milk poured over them. It is a simple yet hearty meal.

Pros: Comforting and wholesome dish, a traditional Slovenian recipe, perfect for breakfast or a light lunch.

Cons: May not appeal to those who are not fond of buckwheat flavor, limited availability outside Slovenia.

Cost: Prices vary depending on the restaurant, ranging from €8 to €15 per plate.

Gibanica:

Gibanica is a layered pastry made from filo dough, filled with a mixture of various ingredients, such as cottage cheese, eggs, poppy seeds, walnuts, and apples. It is a beloved Slovenian dessert.

Pros: Rich and indulgent flavors, a popular traditional dessert, visually appealing presentation.

Cons: Can be quite heavy and sweet for some, and may not suit dietary restrictions.

Cost: Prices vary depending on the bakery or café, ranging from €10 to €20 per gibanica.

This page was left blank intentionally

Conclusion

I'm overcome with happiness and satisfaction as I think back on my trip to Slovenia. It exceeded my expectations and was a truly unforgettable experience. Slovenia has won my heart and given me priceless memories, from the breathtaking natural scenery to the rich cultural heritage. I'll go into detail about my trip's highlights and the reasons you should travel to Slovenia in this final paragraph.

Slovenia is unmatched in its natural beauty, first and foremost. I had the chance to travel to the breathtaking Julian Alps, where I undertook exhilarating hikes and enjoyed panoramic views of towering peaks, glistening lakes, and lush green valleys. The Triglav National Park provided a tranquil retreat into nature with its unspoiled wilderness and varied flora and fauna. With its picturesque island and medieval castle perched on a cliff, the famous Lake Bled offered a picture-perfect setting that seemed too good to be true. The Soa River's emerald waters fascinated me with their vivid color and provided a playground for several water sports. For outdoor enthusiasts and nature lovers, Slovenia's landscapes are a true paradise.

Slovenia has a rich cultural heritage that enthralled me at every turn in addition to its natural beauty. Ljubljana, Slovenia's charming capital, greeted me with its energetic vibe, lively cafes, and stunning architecture. The Ljubljana Castle perched atop a hill, offered sweeping views of the city below and offered a window into the history of the nation. I was transported back in time to a previous era of maritime trade and cross-cultural exchange by the charming coastal town of Piran with its winding narrow streets and Venetian architecture. With its charming old town and well-preserved castle, the medieval town of Ptuj offered a window into Slovenia's past. I came across friendly, welcoming locals everywhere I went who shared their stories and traditions and made me feel like a member of the Slovenian community.

During my trip, Slovenia offered a gastronomic delight that stood out. I savored the culinary delights of the land and sampled traditional foods that exhibited the diversity of Slovenian cuisine. Each bite was a revelation of flavors, from the delicious potica, a rolled pastry filled with a variety of sweet or savory fillings, to the hearty truklji, rolled dumplings filled with cottage cheese or other delectable ingredients. I savored the regional wines, which are prized for their excellence and distinctive qualities, as well as the variety of farm-to-table ingredients, which demonstrated Slovenia's dedication to sustainable and real culinary experiences. I had a real gastronomic adventure in Slovenia, dining in traditional restaurants and learning about regional specialties, and I was left wanting more.

Throughout my trip, I was delighted by the Slovenian people's friendliness and hospitality. I was made to feel welcome and embraced everywhere I went, from the kind locals who led me along hiking trails to the passionate tour guides who shared their knowledge of the nation's history and culture. The commitment of the Slovenian people to protecting the environment and promoting sustainable tourism was evidence of their genuine pride in their nation and a deep appreciation for their natural surroundings. Being a temporary member of their community and witnessing their love for their country were both touching experiences.

In conclusion, my trip to Slovenia was a life-changing experience that will always be etched in my soul. Slovenia is a unique destination because of its outstanding natural beauty, rich cultural heritage, mouthwatering cuisine, and friendly locals. Every moment was filled with wonder and enchantment, whether I was discovering the breathtaking landscapes, learning about the history and customs of the nation, or enjoying the flavors of Slovenian cuisine. Every traveler's bucket list should include Slovenia because it is a hidden gem. It offers a wide variety of experiences as well as a true connection to culture and nature. Slovenia was a dream come true for my vacation, and I can't wait to go back and see even more of this fascinating nation.